Edward Butts

Edward Butts is the author of several published books, most of them historical non-fiction. Many of his books are for adult readers, but he has also written for juveniles. Ed has had three books shortlisted for awards, including *The Desperate Ones*, nominated for an Arthur Ellis Award, and, most recently, *SOS: Stories of Survival*, nominated for a Red Maple Award. He is also the author of a humorous book about English grammar, *Idioms for Aliens*, and has written lyrics for educational songs for children. Ed has previously contributed to the Quest Biography series with *Henry Hudson: New World Voyager*.

Ed has written hundreds of feature-length articles for various publications, including the *Globe and Mail*, *Toronto Star*, and *Old West Magazine*. His articles cover such topics as history, education, entertainment, humour, current events, travel, and writing. He has also written hundreds of short articles on a wide variety of topics — everything from gardening to airlines — for *www. ExquisiteWriting.com*. Ed lives in Guelph, Ontario.

In the same collection

Ven Begamudré, *Isaac Brock: Larger Than Life*
Lynne Bowen, *Robert Dunsmuir: Laird of the Mines*
Kate Braid, *Emily Carr: Rebel Artist*
Edward Butts, *Henry Hudson: New World Voyager*
Anne Cimon, *Susanna Moodie: Pioneer Author*
Deborah Cowley, *Lucille Teasdale: Doctor of Courage*
Gary Evans, *John Grierson: Trailblazer of Documentary Film*
Julie H. Ferguson, *James Douglas: Father of British Columbia*
Judith Fitzgerald, *Marshall McLuhan: Wise Guy*
lian goodall, *William Lyon Mackenzie King: Dreams and Shadows*
Tom Henighan, *Vilhjalmur Stefansson: Arctic Adventurer*
Stephen Eaton Hume, *Frederick Banting: Hero, Healer, Artist*
Naïm Kattan, *A.M. Klein: Poet and Prophet*
Betty Keller, *Pauline Johnson: First Aboriginal Voice of Canada*
Heather Kirk, *Mazo de la Roche: Rich and Famous Writer*
Valerie Knowles, *William C. Van Horne: RailwayTitan*
Vladimir Konieczny, *Glenn Gould: A Musical Force*
Michelle Labrèche-Larouche, *Emma Albani: International Star*
D.H. Lahey, *George Simpson: Blaze of Glory*
Wayne Larsen, *A.Y. Jackson: A Love for the Land*
Wayne Larsen, *James Wilson Morrice: Painter of Light and Shadow*
Wayne Larsen, *Tom Thomson: Artist of the North*
Peggy Dymond Leavey, *Mary Pickford: Canada's Silent Sire, America's Sweetheart*
Francine Legaré, *Samuel de Champlain: Father of New France*
Margaret Macpherson, *Nellie McClung: Voice for the Voiceless*
Nicholas Maes, *Robertson Davies: Magician of Words*
Dave Margoshes, *Tommy Douglas: Building the New Society*
Marguerite Paulin, *René Lévesque: Charismatic Leader*
Raymond Plante, *Jacques Plante: Behind the Mask*
Jim Poling Sr., *Tecumseh: Shooting Star, Crouching Panther*
T.F. Rigelhof, *George Grant: Redefining Canada*
Tom Shardlow, *David Thompson: A Trail by Stars*
Arthur Slade, *John Diefenbaker: An Appointment with Destiny*
Roderick Stewart, *Wilfrid Laurier: A Pledge for Canada*
Sharon Stewart, *Louis Riel: Firebrand*
André Vanasse, *Gabrielle Roy: A Passion for Writing*
John Wilson, *John Franklin: Traveller on Undiscovered Seas*
John Wilson, *Norman Bethune: A Life of Passionate Conviction*
Rachel Wyatt, *Agnes Macphail: Champion of the Underdog*

A QUEST BIOGRAPHY

SIMON GIRTY
WILDERNESS WARRIOR

EDWARD BUTTS

DUNDURN
TORONTO

Copy Editor: Jennifer McKnight
Design: Jesse Hooper
Printer: Webcom

Library and Archives Canada Cataloguing in Publication

Butts, Edward, 1951-
    Simon Girty : wilderness warrior / Edward Butts.

(A Quest biography)
Includes bibliographical references and index.
Issued also in electronic formats.
ISBN 978-1-55488-949-5

    1. Girty, Simon, 1741-1818. 2. Indian agents--Biography. 3. Indians of North America--Wars--1750-1815. 4. Pioneers--Ohio River Valley--Biography. 5. Northwest, Old--History.

I. Title. II. Series: Quest biography

F517.G52B88 2011   977'.02092   C2011-901900-0

1 2 3 4 5   15 14 13 12 11

We acknowledge the support of the **Canada Council for the Arts** and the **Ontario Arts Council** for our publishing program. We also acknowledge the financial support of the **Government of Canada** through the **Canada Book Fund** and **Livres Canada Books**, and the **Government of Ontario** through the **Ontario Book Publishing Tax Credit** and the **Ontario Media Development Corporation**.

Care has been taken to trace the ownership of copyright material used in this book. The author and the publisher welcome any information enabling them to rectify any references or credits in subsequent editions.

J. Kirk Howard, President

Printed and bound in Canada.
www.dundurn.com

Dundurn	Gazelle Book Services Limited	Dundurn
3 Church Street, Suite 500	White Cross Mills	2250 Military Road
Toronto, Ontario, Canada	High Town, Lancaster, England	Tonawanda, NY
M5E 1M2	LA1 4XS	U.S.A. 14150

To the memory of Dwight Girty,
who never gave up on the truth about Simon.

Contents

Acknowledgements

I owe a debt of gratitude to the late Dwight Girty, who helped me more than he ever realized when I was researching the life of his controversial ancestor.

Thanks to Randy Wilkins for the use of the portrait of Simon Girty that appears on the cover, and to Timothy Truman for the use of an illustration from *Wilderness*. I especially thank author Phillip W. Hoffman and publisher David E. Kane of American History Press for the use of Mr. Hoffman's biography *Simon Girty: Turncoat Hero*. The map in this book appears through their courtesy. For other illustrations I thank the Filson Club of Kentucky, the Detroit Public Library, the Ohio Historical Society, the Seneca County Museum of Ohio, the Brant Historical Society, and the Clements Library of Ann Arbor, Michigan.

My thanks to all the people at Dundurn, particularly Kirk Howard, Michael Carroll, and Jennifer McKnight. My thanks also to the Ontario Archives, Library and Archives Canada, and once again to the staff of the Guelph Public library.

Introduction

The following tale was collected by an American student researching Revolutionary War folklore in Pennsylvania. It's typical of the yarns that were once told about one of the most reviled men in North American history. It has a little bit of everything: drama, violence, sneak attacks, kidnapping, a secret hideout, loot, and an outright villain.

Simon Girty was a white renegade that used to raid white settlements about the time of the Revolution. He and his cutthroat Indians would sneak up on a lone cabin, scalp the men, and run off with the women and children. Girty was just plain evil. He and his Indians raided right around Harrisburg and Carlisle. He had an island in the Susquehanna that he used as

> a hideout ... used to bury all the valuables he
> stole from the cabins there. There's a big rock on
> the river they call Girty's Notch. The treasure is
> still there, because Girty was killed in one of his
> own raids and never got a chance to dig it up.

My interest in Simon Girty goes back many years to when I was a mature student in the Department of Integrated Studies at the University of Waterloo. Dr. James Reaney, head of the English Department at the University of Western Ontario, had agreed to be one of my degree supervisors and he suggested Girty as the subject of my degree project. The result was a combined play and essay titled *The Fame of Simon Girty* that examines the life and legend of a man whom the Americans hated even more than Benedict Arnold, but who was a Loyalist hero and a champion of the Native cause. The project not only earned me my degree, but it left me with a fascination with this intriguing individual that continues to this day.

While I was doing research for the project I met Dwight Girty, a resident of Windsor, Ontario, and a direct descendant of Simon. Dwight, who has since passed on, was a senior citizen, but because he had a great interest in his ancestor's story, and had done much research on it himself, he was more than willing to help me with my project. Dwight put me up in his home when I was in Windsor, and for years after my graduation we kept in touch by phone and by mail.

I have long wanted to do a proper biography about Girty — something more objective than the two existing works, *History of the Girtys* (1890) by Consul W. Butterfield, and *Simon Girty, the White Savage* (1928) by Thomas Boyd. Both authors were greatly influenced by prejudiced notions concerning Girty's activities and character. I got started on in-depth research a couple of times, but something always came up to keep me from really getting into it. The best I could manage was a chapter about Girty for *Pirates & Outlaws of Canada*, which I co-authored with Harold Horwood. (Some of the information in that chapter I now know to be inaccurate.)

Then, through Dwight, I became acquainted with American author Phillip W. Hoffman, another man with an enduring passion for the true story of Simon Girty and his contemporaries. Phil had undertaken the very difficult task of researching everything there was to know about Girty and his world. He had compiled such a massive amount of information that I was able to contribute just one or two little tidbits that he didn't already know. After years of hard work, Phil had his book, *Simon Girty: Turncoat Hero*, published in the United States in 2008.

Phil's book is an exciting read, while at the same time being a scholarly account of a man in a time and place of American history that has been wrapped in layer upon layer of myth. When I read the inscribed copy Phil sent me, I thought that I needn't bother trying to do a Girty biography; he had already done a job that could not be surpassed. That was before I became aware of Dundurn's Quest Biography series.

Not long after I received Phil's book, Michael Carroll of Dundurn asked me if I would do a Quest Biography on the explorer Henry Hudson. The result was *Henry Hudson: New World Voyager*, which was published in 2009. Some time later, Michael asked me if I could suggest another Quest subject. I was mulling over possible explorers, soldiers, et cetera, when it struck me that Simon Girty would be a perfect subject. I gave Michael an article on Girty I'd had published several years earlier, and said, "How about him?"

Although I still had all of my old research material on Girty to work with, I used Phil Hoffman's excellent book as a principal source for this Quest Biography. Readers can experience all of the excitement and adventure of Simon Girty's colourful life and gain some perspective on the role he played in early Canadian history. To those who wish to delve into some of the more in-depth aspects of Girty's family and contemporaries, and the time and place in history that they occupied, I highly recommend *Simon Girty: Turncoat Hero.*

Prologue
One Last Act of Defiance

On the morning of July 7, 1796, word spread through the frontier settlement of Detroit that the Americans were coming. Two schooners carrying an advance party of soldiers had been seen on the Detroit River. In accordance with the peace treaty between Great Britain and the United States of America, Detroit and other forts in the Northwest territories held by the British were finally passing into American hands. Not everybody was happy about that.

Many of Detroit's residents had already ferried their families and moveable property across the river to the town of Amherstburg on the Canadian side. Out of spite and anger at losing their Detroit homes to the Americans, they had smashed windows and filled the wells with stones. These people felt that they had been betrayed. Perhaps no one believed that more than a tough, middle-aged frontiersman named Simon Girty. As the American schooners approached the town, Simon was drinking in a tavern. He seemed to be in no hurry to leave, even though the Americans might very well shoot him on sight.

For twenty years Simon had been an implacable foe of the Americans. As far as he was concerned, their desire for independence from Britain had been fueled more by greed for Native lands than by any ideals about liberty. Simon had fought hard against them in the Revolutionary War and in the Indian Wars that followed. Because Simon had been raised by Natives and stood with them as a brother warrior in battle, the Americans called him the "White Savage." Simon was aware of the stories — most of them grossly exaggerated — that were told about him in the American settlements. In tales that parents used to frighten their children into obedience, he was "the Fiend of the Frontier," a "White Beast in human form," the "Great Renegade," or simply "Dirty Girty."

Simon didn't care what the Americans said about him. He had fought bravely and honourably for King George and for his adopted people. Then the British had betrayed him and the Natives. First there had been the stunning news of the British surrender to George Washington and his French allies at Yorktown in 1783. And now, following General Anthony Wayne's crushing defeat of the Natives at the Battle of Fallen Timbers, the British were turning their backs on the Natives. Lands that the tribes considered their own had, with the stroke of a pen, been ceded to the Americans. This was land that many white settlers who had remained loyal to the king considered to be part of the colony of Canada, to which it had been attached after the fall of New France a generation earlier.

As a reward for his long service to the British Indian Department, Simon had been given a tract of farmland near

Amherstburg. He lived there with his wife and children when he wasn't away fighting the Americans or serving as an interpreter at treaty negotiations between the British and the Natives. But the quiet life of a farmer did not agree with Simon. He had always been a man of action. Now, as he drank in the tavern, it galled him that he would no longer be able to cross the river at will. The Americans had declared him an outlaw and put a price on his head. The soldiers who were landing at the wharf would like nothing better than to capture the White Savage and see him hanged, if they didn't shoot him first.

Simon wondered if perhaps he should have taken the early ferry across the river to safety, but he had never been one to just run away from danger. He was going to stay in Detroit until the last possible moment, just to show defiance. The soldiers were now fanning through the town in foot patrols, inspecting the damage done by the previous occupants. Then someone told one of the officers that the notorious Simon Girty was drinking in a nearby tavern.

The officer called to several troopers to follow him, and then raced up the street toward the tavern. This would make him famous. The man who captured the Great Renegade!

The soldiers had the tavern in sight when word reached Simon that the Americans knew he was there. He stepped out the front door. His horse, a white mare that he had ridden for many years, waited at the hitching rail. Simon looked down the street and saw the soldiers. Some of the troopers shouted when they caught sight of him. None of them had ever seen Simon Girty before, but they knew him from the bright red bandana that he wore on his head, pirate fashion. He was almost within musket range.

Suddenly Simon jumped into the saddle. With a whoop he put his heels to the mare and she broke into a gallop, straight for the river. The soldiers gave chase. Even though Simon was mounted and they were afoot, they knew that they could catch him at the riverbank. If he tried to escape by boat they would have him before he could put an oar in the water.

As he tore through the dirt streets of Detroit, Simon hugged the horse's neck so he would make a smaller target if the soldiers opened fire. When he had the wharf in sight, he urged the mare on. The horse did not slow down as her hoofs pounded onto the wooden planking. Before the astonished eyes of the pursuing soldiers, the horse galloped to the end of the wharf and, with a victory cry from Simon, leapt into the air and plunged into the river.

For a moment, man and horse disappeared beneath the surface. Then they came into view, Simon clinging to the horse's back. The river's powerful current was carrying them downstream, but the horse made steady progress toward the Canadian shore. The animal was a strong swimmer and had too much of a head start for the soldiers to have any hope of catching up in a boat. The American officer could only look on in furious disappointment.

When at last the exhausted mare clambered up the riverbank, Simon dismounted. He looked across the river at the land where he had been branded an outlaw and shouted an oath. Of course, the soldiers on the other side were too far away to hear it, but his dramatic escape from right under the noses of the troops would give the Americans something else to talk about — another tale in the saga of the White Savage.

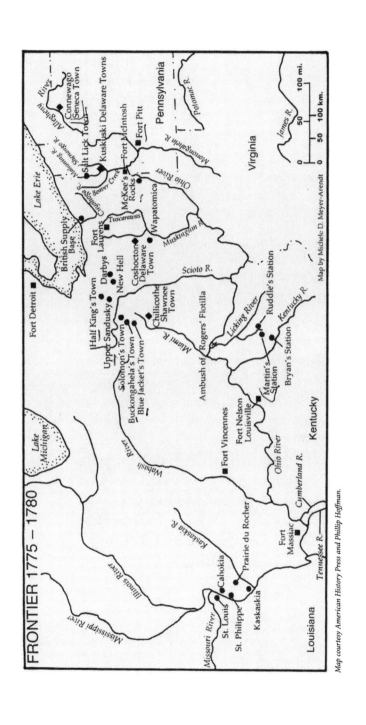

FRONTIER 1775 – 1780

Map courtesy *American History Press* and *Phillip Hoffman.*

Map by Michele D. Meyer-Arendt

1

War Drums

It was the summer of 1756, and fifteen-year-old Simon Girty was among the uneasy settlers crowded into the rough stockade called Fort Granville on the Juniata River in Western Pennsylvania. It was not a comfortable place in which to be confined. Dozens of men, women, and children had to share living space in a relatively small enclosure surrounded by a log palisade. Accommodations were primitive: if you didn't have a place in one of the few cabins, you slept outdoors on the ground. Sanitation was almost non-existent: the privies stank in the summer heat and were thick with flies. The women and older girls divided their time between cooking and looking after the smaller children, who whined from boredom. The men and the older boys like Simon had their share of chores to do in the cramped fort, but they also had to take their turns going on patrols into the forest and keeping watch at the walls. War had come to the Pennsylvania frontier.

Some of Simon's neighbours had already been killed or carried away as prisoners.

Because their homestead was vulnerable to attack, Simon's family had fled to Fort Granville. With him were his mother Mary; brothers Thomas, eighteen; James, twelve; George, ten; half-brother John Turner, eighteen months; and step-father John Turner, who was a sergeant in the local militia. As the teenage boy took his turn standing watch with a musket in his hands, the situation must have been as bewildering to him as it was frightening. The enemies out there in the forest were Delaware warriors — people he had always known as friends.

Simon Girty's father, Simon Sr., an Irish immigrant, had been a fur trader. He'd gone into the business with a prominent merchant named Thomas McKee. Simon Sr. would load up a pack train of up to twenty horses with trade goods that the Natives wanted: steel knives and hatchets, guns, gunpowder and lead, flints, rum, cloth, blankets, coloured beads, traps, silver jewellery, mirrors, and metal cooking pots. He was literally a travelling general store. The Natives paid for his merchandise with animal pelts, particularly deer skins.

Simon Sr. had to travel the forest trails into the valleys of the Allegheny and Ohio Rivers. He competed not only with other traders from the English colonies, but also with French Canadians who followed the river routes from New France in their canoes. It was a risky business, because both the English and the French claimed the territory, and tribes sometimes switched their alliances. He dealt mainly with the Delawares and earned their respect. His reputation as an honest trader spread to other tribes. When Simon Sr. married an English girl named Mary Newton and took up a homestead in Lancaster County, the place soon became a regular stopover for Natives travelling between their home territories and the frontier settlements.

Young Simon, who was born on November 14, 1741, grew up accustomed to being in the company of Natives. They often came to the Girty house to visit his father. Sometimes large delegations of Natives on their way to treaty talks would break their journey at the Girty farm to buy some bread and milk. Little Simon would wander among them, fascinated. The Native leaders wore their finest regalia: shirts embroidered with quill and beadwork. Ornaments of shining silver decorated their bodies. The men wore breechcloths and deerskin leggings. Some warriors carried bows and had quivers full of arrows on their backs. Others had muskets. Tomahawks and knives were looped to their waists by thongs. The women wore calf-length dresses of deerskin or calico. Naked children would run laughing and shouting through the colourful throng.

Simon wasn't afraid of these people, who often gave him and his brothers small gifts. Nor was there any undue concern from his parents. While most of their white settler neighbours feared and hated the Natives, the Girtys did not. To most of the whites on the frontier, the Natives were little more than dangerous beasts who had to be removed so the vast wilderness could be opened to settlement and "civilization." They made no distinctions between the various tribes. It didn't matter to those people if Natives were Iroquois, Delaware, or Shawnee — they were all "savages." Traders like Simon Sr. were regarded by their fellow whites with a certain degree of suspicion because they travelled into mysterious and dangerous "Indian country." Because the Girtys even welcomed Natives at their home as guests, neighbours branded the family as "Injun lovers." It was intended as an insult, but it did not bother young Simon.

Disaster struck the family late in 1750 when Simon Sr. was killed in a fight with a man named Samuel Saunders, who was subsequently sent to prison for manslaughter. Mary Girty was now left with four boys to care for, ranging in age from four to eleven. But, like most pioneer families, the Girtys were hardy and independent. Simon, Thomas, and James helped their mother plough the fields and harvest the crops. While James played with little George so their mother could tend to chores, Thomas and Simon hunted for game. Simon already knew a few tricks of woodcraft that he'd learned from Native friends.

Meanwhile, a farmer named John Turner took an interest in Mary Girty. He was hard-working, good natured, and the Girty

Photo courtesy of the Filson Club, Louisville, Kentucky.

Boonesborough, founded by Daniel Boone, was a typical frontier fortified community. Fort Granville, where the Girty-Turner family was captured, would have looked very much like it.

boys liked him. Three years after the death of Simon Sr., Mary married John Turner. In February 1755, she gave birth to her fifth son, John Turner Jr. But the happiness of the Girty-Turner family was short-lived. War drums were pounding in the forests of the frontier.

At the strategic point where the Allegheny and Monongahela Rivers converge to form the Ohio River, the French had built a new stronghold called Fort Duquesne. The British colony of Pennsylvania had just purchased a huge parcel of land from the Iroquois Six Nations Confederacy. As far as the British were concerned, Fort Duquesne was on their property. French and English interests in the territory had been on a collision course for a long time. Now the clash was about to come.

In the summer of 1755 a British general, Edward Braddock, led a force of regular British troops and colonial militia against Fort Duquesne. Among his officers was a young George Washington, and one of his wagon drivers was a twenty-one-year-old frontiersman named Daniel Boone. General Braddock was fresh from England and had no experience whatsoever at wilderness warfare. He refused to listen to the advice of his colonial officers. On July 9, he led his army right into an ambush a few miles from Fort Duquesne.

A few hundred French troops and Canadian militiamen, and about a thousand of their Native allies, literally cut the British army to pieces. Over nine hundred men, including General Braddock, were killed. Many British soldiers were taken prisoner and died at the torture stake. Washington and Boone were among those who escaped the slaughter.

It now appeared to many of the tribes that the French were the superior power. Emboldened by the spectacular defeat of a British army, and urged on by the French, Delaware raiding parties struck at the more isolated homesteads, killing, scalping, burning, and carrying off captives. Some of the raids took place near John Turner's farm. Turner joined the militia and helped build Fort Granville. In the spring of 1756, a series of deadly raids on outlying farms kept the region in a state of alarm. Turner decided to take his family to the safety of the fort.

Days passed and nothing happened. One night, as they lay on the ground beside the glowing remains of a cooking fire, unable to sleep, James asked Simon, "Why do you suppose the Delawares are on the warpath against us? They used to come to the house when Pa was alive, and they acted like we was all kin. Now all of a sudden, they want to kill us. Why?"

"I don't exactly know, James," Simon replied. "I think they liked Pa because he didn't try to cheat them, like lot of the other traders do. But do you remember all that trouble when Pa tried to set up a trading post right in Delaware country? They sure got mad, and Pa had to get out quick. The way I see it, the Delawares and all the rest of them stop being friendly as soon as white folks start moving into their country like they mean to stay."

Then Thomas's voice came from the other side of the fire, where the eldest Girty brother lay wrapped in a blanket. "Injuns are savages, Simon. You can't trust them. I used to think otherwise, but I know better now."

On July 22, there was a general alarm when a bloody and breathless man stumbled into the fort. He had been attacked in the woods and barely escaped with his life. Captain Edward Ward, the fort's commander, ordered the gates closed and barred. Men rushed to the walls and primed their guns.

Watching through a loophole, Simon saw about sixty Delaware warriors emerge from the forest into the clearing that surrounded the fort. Staying just out of firing range, they shouted insults and challenged the men to come out and fight. A few of the warriors turned and flaunted their bare backsides. Simon knew that this was their way of showing their contempt for an enemy. It was meant to anger the fort's defenders and draw them out, but Captain Ward wouldn't take the bait. His men stayed in the fort, and the Delawares withdrew back into the forest.

The wary captain wanted the people to stay in the fort, but after a few days, when it seemed that the Delawares had surely gone, many of the farmers became concerned about their crops. It was time to harvest the early wheat and oats. They wanted armed escorts so they could bring in their grain. Ward didn't like the idea, but at last he gave in to their arguments. He led most of the militiamen out of the fort to protect the harvesters. Now only twenty-four men were left in the fort. One of them was John Turner.

On August 2, a company of fifty-five French soldiers commanded by Captain Louis Coulon de Villiers and about a hundred Delaware warriors attacked Fort Granville. Captain Ward and his men were too far away to even hear the shooting. For a day and a night the fort's outnumbered defenders kept the enemy at bay. Older boys like Simon and Thomas were assigned loopholes to shoot through. However, in spite of the brave defence, the attackers got close enough to set part of the wooden palisade on fire. Several men who tried to extinguish the blaze were shot. One was a lieutenant named Armstrong whom Ward had left in command. The situation in the fort was now hopeless.

On the morning of August 3, Captain de Villiers called out that if the fort were surrendered immediately, the defenders would be given quarter — otherwise there would be a massacre. Lieutenant Armstrong's death had left Sergeant John Turner in charge. Realizing that he had no choice, Turner opened the gate.

The victorious French and Delawares pillaged the fort of flour, gunpowder, and anything else of value that could be carried off. Then they burned the stockade down. Simon and the rest of the prisoners were forced to carry the plunder like pack horses. The journey to Fort Duquesne was an ordeal that lasted about a fortnight. The prisoners with their heavy burdens were hurried along and warned that if they fell behind or tried to escape, they would be killed on the spot. Simon saw this threat made good when they were joined by another war party that had prisoners. One man was too weak to keep up, so a warrior tomahawked and scalped him.

When the warriors and their captives reached Fort Duquesne, John Turner hoped that all of the prisoners would be taken into the custody of the French. They might then be sent to Quebec where they would be held until they were repatriated in a prisoner exchange with the British. But this was not to be. Part of the Delawares' reward for assisting the French was to do as they pleased with prisoners.

The captives were taken to the Delaware town of Kittanning on the Allegheny River. There, on the orders of a war chief, John Turner was separated from the rest and marked for death. Some of the warriors at Kittanning were old friends of Simon Sr. They had heard that he had been killed by another white man. They recognized Mary and the Girty boys, and decided that Turner had killed Simon Sr. in order to steal his wife. No amount of argument would change their minds, so before the very eyes of his wife and stepsons, John Turner was tortured to death. For the Girty boys to have to watch the man who had shown them nothing but kindness die slowly and in agony must have been emotionally and psychologically devastating.

Not long after the death of her second husband, Mary Girty-Turner and her baby son John were given to a party of Shawnees who took them to one of their villages on the Scioto River. Several other prisoners were tomahawked and scalped, but no physical harm was done to the Girty brothers. They were looked upon as good candidates for adoption, but that did not mean they were out of danger. At any moment, a member of the tribe who had lost a loved one in war with the whites could demand the life of a white prisoner as retribution.

Thomas, Simon, James, and George were treated well. They were fed, given shelter, and were relatively free to move around in the village. They were on their honour not to attempt to escape. If they tried to run, and were recaptured, they would suffer the same awful fate as John Turner.

During those first weeks of captivity, while the Girty brothers were undergoing the initial steps of Native resocialization, back in the settlements a retaliatory force was being raised by Colonel John Armstrong, brother of the lieutenant who had been killed at Fort Granville. The target was Kittanning, where Armstrong planned to strike a punitive blow against the Delawares and rescue white captives. Unlike the bungling General Braddock, Colonel Armstrong knew how to fight the Natives on their own ground. His force of frontier militiamen advanced on the Delaware town undetected. Early on the morning of September 8, they attacked.

The militiamen opened fire on the village, taking the Delawares completely by surprise. Warriors quickly rushed to defend the perimeter, while women and children fled into the woods. Simon, James, and George were quickly seized and forced to run with them, not having the slightest chance to make a break for the militia lines. However, Thomas was in a different part of the camp. He and several other prisoners made a run for it. All around them the air was filled with the crack of gunfire and the battle cries of both whites and Natives. Some of the Delaware houses were on fire, and the smoke mixed with the clouds of gunsmoke. There was an ear-splitting blast as a keg of gunpowder in one of the burning houses exploded. The resulting confusion gave Thomas the chance he needed to make it to Colonel Armstrong's men. Not all of the prisoners who had tried to flee were so lucky.

The militiamen withdrew, leaving Kittanning in flames. They had killed between thirty and forty warriors, as well as a number of women and children. Eleven prisoners, including Thomas Girty, had been rescued. The eldest Girty brother had no idea of the fate of Simon, James, and George.

2

Captivity

Fifteen-year-old Simon Girty had never felt so alone or so afraid. He was about to be subjected to a brutal test of courage and endurance upon which his very life might depend. Whatever emotions churned inside him, the boy held them in. He set his face in an expression of grim determination. Simon had learned that his captors would interpret any show of fear as a sign of weakness. That could result in a quick death from a tomahawk blow to the head, or a slow one at the torture stake.

Simon had made up his mind that, no matter what it took, he was going to survive. His father had been murdered and his stepfather cruelly executed. His mother and baby half-brother John were somewhere in Shawnee territory. Thomas had escaped. After the battle at Kittanning, the Delawares had given twelve-year-old James to a party of Shawnee warriors. The Delawares had decided to keep ten-year-old George with them, but had given Simon to a band of Senecas.

Simon didn't know if he would ever see any of his family again, but in spite of all the horrors he had experienced, he knew he was lucky to be alive. Other captives had felt the wrath of the Delawares after the destruction of Kittanning.

Now, in the autumn of 1756, Simon was in a Seneca village on the south shore of the eastern end of Lake Erie. He was among a strange people and farther from home than he had ever been. The journey from Kittanning had been a rough lesson in the ways of warriors on the trail. The men travelled quickly along the forest paths, pausing only to sleep and eat their trail rations of nuts, dried berries, and smoked meat. They had been impressed with young Simon's stamina in keeping up with them, and the fact that he never complained. They contemptuously threw away his hard-soled shoes and gave him a pair of soft deerhide moccasins. When they made camp at night, the warriors took time to teach him some Seneca words, and expressed great pleasure at how quickly he learned them. Some of his captors spoke broken English, but it was essential that he learn their language quickly if he wanted to win their favour.

Simon had been around Natives enough to know that adoption of captives was common. Some of the Natives who had visited the Girty farm had been adopted into tribes that had captured them in raids. However, before a male captive could be deemed worthy of adoption, there was a test. The gauntlet!

To prove himself, Simon would have to run between two long rows of men, women, and children who were armed with whips and clubs. He had been stripped naked for the ordeal, so that no part of his body had any protection. If he could reach the pole at the far end of the gauntlet, he would be worthy of adoption, but if he fell and couldn't get back up, he would be dead within the hour.

Simon stood a few feet from the waiting lines of Senecas. He could feel all of their eyes on him. He tried to ignore their faces and concentrate on the pole at the far end. It seemed impossibly far away. All of those pairs of hands in between, waiting to strike him down!

Simon was a strong youth, stockily built, and toughened by a boyhood of hard work. He was sure he could take a lot of punishment without collapsing. His greatest fear was of being stunned by a blow to the head. That would finish him.

Before he lurched into his run, Simon suddenly bent over from the waist, with his chin tucked into his chest. He was looking at the ground, but could see just far enough ahead to keep himself in the right direction. He crossed his arms over the top of his head, and balled his hands into fists. He couldn't run his fastest in this position, but his head and his face were protected and it would be difficult for anyone to land a solid blow on those other vulnerable parts of his body: his abdomen and groin.

Simon bulled his way down the gauntlet. Clubs struck hard on his back and his buttocks. He felt the sting of whips on his thighs and calves. But blows that were aimed at his head or face hit his arms and hands. They hurt, but he was still on his feet. All the while the men yelled their war whoops, the women ululated, and the children shrieked with laughter.

As the blows rained down, Simon clenched his teeth against the pain and kept putting one foot in front of the other. He couldn't tell when he passed the halfway point; he just knew that he was beginning to stagger. Maybe he wouldn't make it after all. Then suddenly a loud cry went up from the Senecas, and Simon realized that nobody was hitting him anymore. He looked up, and saw the post in front of him. Another step and he'd run into it. Simon might have collapsed then, but a pair of warriors hoisted him onto their shoulders to parade him around the village in triumph.

Simon was battered and bruised and he had welts and cuts where the whips had hit him, but his initiation into the Seneca tribe was not over. First some women dragged him into the lake and ritualistically scrubbed him to wash the "whiteness" out of him. Then he had to sit and not cry out as an elderly warrior plucked the hair out of his head until he was bald, except for a scalplock on his crown. This was tied with a bit of red ribbon. Finally he was given clothing appropriate for a Seneca youth: breechcloth and leggings, a deerskin shirt, and moccasins.

Simon Girty was now a member of one of the most powerful tribes in the Northwest. The Senecas were the westernmost of the Iroquois Six Nations Confederacy. The others were the Cayugas, Onondagas, Oneidas, Tuscaroras, and Mohawks. The Senecas were called "The Keepers of the Western Door," as they guarded the Confederacy against attack from the west. Seneca warriors were feared far and wide and had battled both the English and the French. In the power struggle over the Northwest, both colonial powers had tried to win the Senecas over as allies.

Simon was taken in as a son by a Seneca family. He might have lived in a traditional longhouse — the communal dwelling shared by several families — or his home might have been a cabin, which many Natives of the region were building after the fashion of the white settlers.

The Senecas were farmers and hunters. The women and girls tended the cornfields, vegetable gardens, and orchards. The men and boys hunted and fished. The people had also taken up the white practice of raising cattle, hogs, and poultry.

To most of the white settlers on the frontier, the Natives were, without exception, a barbarous, cruel race, hardly even to be regarded as human. The very idea of being kept in captivity by these forest people was perceived with such horror among the whites that death was considered the better option.

As a member of the Seneca nation, Simon saw a people who were very different from the nightmarish image of blood-thirsty warriors who killed and scalped their victims and burned helpless prisoners at the stake. He was now part of a society in which women owned property and had political power, which was not true of white society. In fact, Seneca society was matriarchal, meaning that women were the heads of families and bloodlines were traced through mothers, not fathers. Although sachems and councils of males made up the Seneca government, it was the women who elected the sachems. Women could even veto a council's decision to go to war simply by withholding the supplies the men needed to take on the warpath.

At the time that Simon became a Seneca, one of their principal chiefs was a man named Guyasuta (also called Kayashota and Kiasutha). He had been one of the leaders who had defeated General Braddock. There is evidence that this exceptional Seneca chief was Simon's mentor, and perhaps even his adopted father. Under Guyasuta's tutelage, Simon would have learned that as a Seneca he was now a brother to all Iroquois. He would have been taught to value honesty, responsibility, and loyalty. In Seneca philosophy, people were more valued than material possessions. Hospitality was an important aspect of everyday life. One was expected to cheerfully share food with visitors. If a person should be wronged, the matter could usually be settled by the guilty party giving the offended party gifts. In the case of murder, justice was carried out by the victim's family. Rape, even of female captives, was punishable by death.

Like many other children in frontier settlements, Simon had never been to school. He could not read nor write. But with Guyasuta and other warriors as his teachers, he received the kind of education he would need to survive in the wilderness. Simon could hunt with the gun and the bow, and he learned to read a trail the way other youths his age could read a book. He could move through the forest as silently as fog, and endure pain, cold, and hunger without complaint.

As he became accustomed to their ways, Simon made many friends among the Senecas. He had a pleasant nature and the other youths enjoyed his company. He found that the Seneca boys liked to laugh and joke, just like the white boys back in the settlements. As the months passed, Simon thought less and less of somehow returning to his own people. Even though he never gave up hope of one day seeing his mother and brothers, he came to accept the Senecas as his people.

Simon learned the Seneca language in a remarkably short time. As he conversed with visitors from other communities of the Six Nations, he began to understand that the Seneca tongue was just a dialect of the larger Iroquoian language group. Simon discovered that he had a gift for learning languages, and in this he was encouraged by Guyasuta. In a land where many Native languages were spoken, not to mention the English and French of the white men, good interpreters were important. A misinterpreted phrase at a treaty negotiation could have disastrous results. In time, Simon would be fluent in at least nine Native languages, and perhaps as many as eleven.

If there was one thing the Iroquois valued as much as courage, it was oratory. It was said to have been the eloquence of the legendary Hiawatha that had brought the Iroquois Confederacy together centuries earlier. A chief who could move people with the power of words was held in as high esteem as a renowned warrior. Moreover, a people who had no written language relied upon the memories of storytellers to keep alive their history, legends, fables, and prayers. This knowledge had to be passed on by means of powerful oratorical skills from one generation to the next so that it was imbedded in the collective memory of the people.

Just as exceptionally bright pupils in the schools back in the settlements were quick to understand the curriculum taught in the classrooms, young Simon proved to be an extraordinary student of the art of verbal communication. He learned to listen carefully, memorize every word while noting pauses and inflections, translate it, and then repeat what had been said. With his sharp, well-trained memory, and his natural skills as an orator, Simon could accurately repeat a speech or a complicated message weeks after he'd heard it. Guyasuta must have been very pleased with his protégé.

Beyond the Seneca country, world-shaking events were taking place that would bring about another profound change in the life of Simon Girty. The French and English, and their respective Native allies, continued their bloody struggle for control of not just the Northwest territory, but all of North America. Guyasuta and his warriors fought for the French against British troops and the colonial militiamen the Natives now called the Long Knives. Simon and other adopted whites took no part in the fighting. The Natives would not force an adopted member of the tribe to go to war against his former people and face the prospect of having to kill a blood relative.

The tide of the war in the Northwest turned against the French in 1758 when the British captured and destroyed Fort Duquesne. They would soon replace it with their own stronghold, Fort Pitt.

Then in 1759 the mighty fortress of Quebec fell. A year later the British captured Montreal and Canada effectively became a British colony. The British looked upon the trans-Appalachian West as an extension of Canada.

Natives who had been allied with the French now had no choice but to make peace with the British if they wanted to get such trade goods as gunpowder and lead. To show their goodwill, they began to return white captives. The Delawares and Shawnees turned over more than three hundred people to George Crogan, the British Deputy Indian Agent at Fort Pitt. One of them was Mary Girty-Turner. However, her young son, John Jr., was still with the Shawnees. Mary took up residence with Thomas at a place near Fort Pitt called Squirrel Hill.

Living in Guyasuta's Seneca town, Simon, who was now a young man, saw what effects the British victory had on his adopted people. There was shock and painful disappointment at the news of the French surrender. Guyasuta was sure that the setback was temporary and that one day the French would return, but, in the meantime, he had to make peace with the British. He was glad when British officers told him that they did not intend to keep their redcoat soldiers in the western forts they had captured from the French. Because the French had been defeated, the British said, the forts would be abandoned. The soldiers would leave.

But the soldiers didn't leave. They remained on Native territory. Even worse, settlers now began crossing the mountains to homestead on land that wasn't theirs. White hunters decimated the deer population. The Natives depended on the deer for meat, but the whites were killing them for the hides. The short-sighted British administration of General Jeffrey Amherst added insult to injury when it placed severe limits on the guns and ammunition Natives could purchase and refused to follow the French practice of offering Native hunters and trappers gifts and credit.

By the spring of 1763, Guyasuta was thoroughly disgusted with the British, whom he accused of treating the Natives like dogs. He joined the Ottawa chief Pontiac in a war to drive them out of the Northwest. The warriors captured several small forts and killed hundreds of British soldiers. They killed an even greater number of settlers and took many prisoners, but they could not capture the main British strongholds of Fort Pitt or Detroit. After more than a year of bloodshed, even though Pontiac stayed on the warpath, Guyasuta and other Native leaders agreed to meet British negotiators at a peace council. One of the conditions to which the Natives had to agree was the return of all white captives, including those who had been adopted.

Simon was devastated when Guyasuta told him that he must go to Fort Pitt and live with the white men. Was he not a Seneca warrior? Had he not earned the right to live among Guyasuta's people?

Guyasuta replied that Simon was indeed a Seneca warrior and he had more than proven himself worthy, but the treaty with the British allowed no exceptions. *All* white captives had to be returned. He told Simon that he must have a strong heart and bear himself like a man. And since he was a man and not a child, once he had returned to Fort Pitt and fulfilled the agreement he would be free to do what he wanted. He did not have to stay there. But, Guyasuta added, it would please him to know that he had a brother Seneca living among the whites at Fort Pitt. For even though there was peace along the frontier at the moment, who knew what tomorrow might bring?

A British officer, Colonel Henry Bouquet, had camped with a force of 1,500 men at the old Wyandot town of Conchake on the Tuscarawas River. It was there that the Senecas, Delawares, and Shawnees were to deliver their captives. Guyasuta and an escort of warriors arrived on November 14, 1764, with a group of captives that included Simon Girty. They found Conchake to be an emotionally charged place.

Tribesmen and their captives had been coming into the town since late October. White people from the settlements had come with Colonel Bouquet to look among the captives for missing family members. There were scenes of great joy when husbands found wives who had been carried off years before, and parents were reunited with children they had feared they might never see again. Some captives wept with happiness to be once again in the arms of loved ones.

But not all of the captives wanted to go back. Some who had been taken years before when they were small children could remember nothing of their former lives and families. They had forgotten how to speak English. They wailed at being taken away from the Native parents who had adopted them. Those parents were just as heartbroken at having to give them up. Some of the white

Colonel Henry Bouquet required the Natives to return all captives. White children were often reluctant to leave their adopted parents.

women had married Native men and had small children. Warrior fathers wept openly as they said goodbye to their little sons and daughters, and pleaded with Colonel Bouquet to be sure that the children were protected and cared for. Some returned captives had to be bound to prevent them from running away to rejoin their Native families.

Amidst all this joy and pathos, Guyasuta took Simon directly to the Assistant Deputy Agent for the British Indian Department, who was documenting the proceedings for Sir William Johnson, the Superintendent of Indian Affairs. The Assistant Deputy Agent was twenty-nine-year-old Lieutenant Alexander McKee, the son of Simon, Sr.'s old business associate Thomas McKee.

Simon and Alex had likely known each other years before when they were boys, but the young man who now stood before McKee did not look like the teenager who had been carried off into the wilderness eight years ago. Simon was now twenty-three-years old. He stood only about five-foot-nine in his moccasins, but had a stocky, muscular body. His head was plucked bare in the Seneca style, except for a scalplock of jet black hair that was tied with a beaded red ribbon. For this important occasion, Simon was dressed in his finest clothes; a deerskin shirt, breechcloth and leggings, all beautifully decorated with quill and bead work. Small silver rings hung from his earlobes. Simon's face was somewhat round and ruggedly handsome. Most notable were his eyes. Simon's eyes were so dark, they were almost black. They were intense eyes that looked as though they could transfix a person and see right into the soul.

Guyasuta told McKee how Simon had come to be with the Seneca. He praised him as a strong, brave, and honest young man of exceptionally good character. Then Guyasuta gave the information that he knew would be of particular interest to McKee and the British Indian Department — Simon could speak more Native languages than any other white man on the frontier! McKee, who spoke fluent Shawnee, was impressed.

Even though Simon knew that he would most likely see Guyasuta again, he nonetheless felt, when the chief left for the Seneca country without him, that he was saying goodbye to a way of life. For eight years he had been a Seneca. Now he was being told that he must become a white man again. He wondered if he could ever entirely be either one.

Simon had a strong urge to get on the horse Guyasuta had given him as a parting gift and follow the chief down the trail. Then he heard McKee call to him from the front of his tent. Simon strode over and entered as McKee stepped aside and held the flap open for him. What he saw caused him to stop in his tracks.

Standing in front of McKee's desk was a tall, slim young man. He was dressed in clothing that Simon instantly recognized as being of Shawnee design. But his blue eyes and fair skin and hair gave him away as a white man. It had been eight years since they had last seen each other at Kittanning, but there was no mistaking a little brother. Simon gasped, "James!"

3

Fort Pitt

Simon and James arrived at Fort Pitt and were happy to learn that their mother and Thomas were living at Squirrel Hill, where Thomas had a prosperous farm. George had been returned by the Delawares and was there with them. When Simon and James showed up at the door, there was a great celebration. The only thing that kept their happiness from being complete was the fact that no one knew the whereabouts of John Turner Jr.

Most of the white people in the vicinity of Fort Pitt mistrusted and even hated Natives. It did not take long for Simon to become aware that he, James, and George were regarded with a degree of suspicion, and were called the "Injun Girtys" behind their backs. Thomas shared his neighbours' dislike of Natives, but he didn't let that come between him and his brothers. As he saw things, it was not their fault that they had not been able to escape, as he had done. Still, when his three brothers "talked

Indian," he knew that they had been part of a world that he could never understand, and did not want to understand.

The three brothers tried to fit in. It was difficult, though, especially for George. He had been only ten at the time of his capture. Now he was eighteen, and had spent almost half of his life as a Delaware. Even though they let their hair grow back and wore "civilized" clothing, there was still one thing that would forever set them apart. They actually *liked* Natives, in spite of all that had happened to them.

When Thomas announced that he was getting married, his brothers built a large log house for themselves and their mother so that they wouldn't be an imposition on Thomas and his bride. They claimed several hundred acres of land and cleared it for farming. But Simon, James, and George were not farmers. With Thomas's agreement, they let him manage their land. They had plenty to keep them busy in Fort Pitt.

The steady stream of Native leaders into Fort Pitt meant that Alex McKee and George Crogan frequently hired the Girty brothers as interpreters. The two Indian Department officers were especially impressed with Simon. Not only was he fluent in a wide range of languages and dialects, he also had a deep understanding of Native politics, culture, religion, and system of values. Moreover, Simon had detailed knowledge of the family connections that existed amongst the many tribes.

Natives in the Ohio Valley and adjacent territories who wanted to trade with the British had to go to Fort Pitt. Some of the leaders, Guyasuta among them, complained that they had to travel long distances. They also said that Fort Pitt was becoming a dangerous place for them, surrounded as it was by settlers who were avowed "Indian haters." They wanted the British to reopen full trade and send traders into their territories.

No doubt it pleased Guyasuta to see Simon employed as a translator at such important talks, but he did not like Crogan's response to the request for traders. Pontiac and his followers were still making war, Crogan said. He would not allow full trade to resume until all hostilities ceased. Moreover, he believed there were still white captives who had not been repatriated.

As a show of goodwill, in May of 1765, the Shawnees brought in a group of more than forty captives and turned them over to Crogan. The Girty brothers were present as interpreters, and one boy caught their attention. He was tall and slender, and appeared to be about eleven years old. The Shawnees called him Theecheapie. They couldn't remember his English name. He had been taken in Pennsylvania about ten years earlier, they said. He didn't speak any English.

The boy had a dark complexion, brown eyes, and long black hair. He could easily have been a full-blooded Native. But something about his looks intrigued the Girtys. They sent for their mother. Mary knelt in front of the boy and looked into his eyes. Then she burst into tears. She had found John Jr. at last.

Young John had no memory of his mother or his half-brothers. But his transition to a new life was made easier by the fact that people in the family spoke Shawnee. Simon took a special interest in the boy, and the two of them became close.

That summer Pontiac finally understood the futility of continuing his war against the British. He accepted Crogan's peace terms. Now that there was no danger of attacks by the Natives, a vast territory lay open for traders. Fort Pitt became a thriving commercial centre as merchants from Philadelphia flocked there to get in on the trading boom. These business-men needed frontiersmen like the Girty brothers not only as interpreters, but also as guides. Nobody in Fort Pitt knew the forest trails and the water routes better than these young men who had lived for so many years in "Indian country."

Simon had found that Alex McKee was one man who did not look down on the "Injun Girtys." McKee, it turned out, had learned to speak Shawnee from his mother. Alex was never clear about whether his mother had been a white captive among the Shawnee, or a full-blooded Native.

One day McKee introduced Simon and James to two men. One was a young businessman from Philadelphia named George Morgan, who had come to Fort Pitt to open an office for his trading firm. He envisioned a commercial empire that would reach deep into Native territory. Morgan would bring in cheap trade goods from Philadelphia, warehouse them at Fort Pitt, and distribute them far and wide among the tribes. His traders would bring furs and hides back to Fort Pitt, to be transported to Philadelphia. The profits would be enormous.

The other man was Matthew Elliott. This short, pug-nosed young Irishman was a born adventurer. Like the Girtys' Irish father, Elliott had established himself as a trader. He'd worked among the Delawares and the Shawnees, and gained their trust and respect. He had even married a Shawnee woman. During the Pontiac War, Elliott had served with McKee under Colonel Bouquet. Now Elliott was working with McKee.

Through Morgan and Elliott, James and Simon met many other men who were gathering at Fort Pitt. These men were of a breed apart from farmers like Thomas Girty. They were hunters, trappers, traders, and river men. A few were French-Canadian *coureurs-de-bois* (runners of the woods). Most of them had lived in close proximity with Natives for years. Some had even been captives. They were tough individualists who preferred the wilderness to towns. They scorned settlers as people who cut down the forests and drove away the game. Simon and James felt right at home in their company.

One thing that these rugged frontiersmen admired was skill with a new type of gun that had recently arrived on the frontier. It was called a rifle, because its barrel had a spiraled bore, instead of the smooth bore of a musket. This innovation gave the gun greater accuracy. Its long barrel — more than four feet — gave it more than twice the range of a musket. A good marksman could bring down a deer at three hundred yards. When frontiersmen got together, shooting contests were almost inevitable, and the Girty brothers showed that they could shoot with the best of them.

George Morgan had thought of another business venture, for which he needed men who could shoot well. Far to the southwest, in the lands that the Shawnees and the Cherokees called *Kenhtake* (Kentucky) and *Tanasi* (Tennessee), the woods were thick with deer. In the meadows and canebrakes there were great numbers of bison, which the frontiersmen called buffalo. Morgan wanted to send boatloads of hunters into those territories to harvest the animals for their hides, meat, and tallow (fat used for making soap and candles). The meat (preserved with salt) and the tallow would be packed in sealed barrels. Using the river routes, the hunters would ship the hides and tallow back to Fort Pitt. Some of the meat would be distributed among the British forts as food for the garrisons, for which Morgan had a contract with the army. The rest would be sent down the Mississippi River to New Orleans for shipment to British colonies in the Caribbean.

Simon liked the idea of being a long hunter, the name given to the men who went on hunting trips that took them far from home for extended periods of time. Early in the summer of 1768, he went to the settlement of Kaskasia, located on the Mississippi at the mouth of the Kaskasia River, where Morgan was outfitting expeditions. Morgan made Simon foreman of a boat with a crew of twenty men. They set off down the Mississippi, and then turned up the Cumberland River to penetrate into the game-rich country. Another boat in the charge of a man named Joseph Hollingshead was to follow in two or three days and rendezvous with Simon's party about three hundred miles up the Cumberland.

The hunting along the Cumberland River was as good as Morgan had said it would be. Simon's men soon had their boat half-filled with buffalo hides, bundles of deerskins, and barrels of salted meat. When the men camped at night, they feasted on a delicacy — roasted buffalo tongue.

Simon learned that the big, shaggy animals weren't easy to bring down. Even after being shot, an enraged bull could charge a man and gore him with its horns. His men had a few close calls.

As they progressed up the Cumberland, the men kept a wary eye for any sign of Natives. Simon knew that they were trespassing on the favourite hunting grounds of the Shawnees, Chickasaws, and Cherokees. Those people were not Simon's Iroquois brothers. He owed them no allegiance, and neither he nor his men could expect any mercy if they were caught.

One day in the first week of July, the men went ashore to hunt. A few stayed at the riverbank to make camp, while the others set off in two groups to search for game. Simon and the half dozen men with him had hardly separated from the others, when the air was suddenly filled with battle cries and the roar of musket fire. A Shawnee war party of at least thirty men burst from concealment and fell upon the hunters. The attack came so swiftly, several of them were cut down before they could defend themselves. Simon saw instantly that his party was cut off from the river. There was nothing they could do but run.

As they dashed through the bush, Simon yelled, "Split up!" These were veteran woodsmen who knew that by taking different directions they might confuse pursuers. It was every man for himself.

Now Simon was running alone. He quickly realized that a party of Shawnees was hot on his heels. He ran faster. But he was not fleeing in blind panic. Simon knew that the Shawnees expected him to run until he dropped from exhaustion. They didn't know that he was a Seneca warrior.

Simon sprinted across a small clearing and then ducked behind a large tree. He cocked the hammer of his rifle and checked the priming. Then he raised the weapon and looked down the gunsights, back across the clearing.

The leading Shawnee warrior came into view at a loping run, easily following Simon's trail. Simon took careful aim and squeezed the trigger. There was a crack of gunfire, a puff of white smoke, and the warrior dropped to the ground.

Simon quickly reloaded. Then he ran to another place where he could lie in ambush. He watched his back trail for more than an hour, but no pursuers appeared. He decided that the other Shawnees must have found their slain comrade and called off the chase.

Simon carefully made his way back to the site of the surprise attack. The ground was littered with the scalped bodies of his men. At the riverside he found his boat smashed-in and useless. The meat and hides had been tossed into the river. There was no sign of any of the men who had fled into the woods with him.

Simon's safest option would have been to quietly make his way alone overland to Fort Pitt. Instead, he chose to take the dangerous route downriver to find Holingshead's party and warn them. Simon then made an incredible journey of more than three hundred miles in two weeks. No sooner did Simon reach Kaskasia, than Morgan sent him back into the forest to search for two missing hunters. In his report, Morgan wrote that Simon found the men, "strolling up and down the Woods they knew not Where."

Morgan had nothing but praise for Simon's courage in warning Holingshead and then finding the lost hunters. But the attack on the hunting party had been a disaster. Morgan had to give up on the meat and hides operation. Out of a job, Simon returned to Fort Pitt. By now the people in the growing settlement were calling it by a new name: Pittsburgh.

4

Border Troubles

Pittsburgh was a bustling frontier town where frock-coated businessmen mingled with woodsmen that Eastern journalists would eventually dub "leather stockings" because of their buckskin clothing. It was a transportation hub for river routes and woodland roads — though the latter were sometimes little more than "Indian trails." All roads led to Pittsburg from the wilds of Kentucky, the Seneca lands on the shore of Lake Erie, and the city of Philadelphia.

In spite of his love for the wilderness, Simon enjoyed rugged Pittsburgh. He liked to sit in the taverns and have a drink with anyone willing to engage in friendly conversation. He was a gifted storyteller, and he liked to hear about others' experiences. People who knew him at this time described him as an outspoken but good-natured man. If he had rough ways, then he was typical of most of the frontiersmen who visited Pittsburg.

Nonetheless, Simon also gained a reputation as a bad man to cross. He could be quarrelsome with people he didn't like, especially when he was drinking.

The end of Pontiac's War did not mean that whites and Natives were living in harmony. The King's Proclamation of 1763 prohibited settlement on lands between the Allegheny Mountains and the Ohio River. That vast, rich country was to remain tribal hunting grounds, but hordes of settlers ignored the proclamation and poured across the mountains to squat illegally on prime land. Leaders like Guyasuta watched with increasing anger as British authorities failed to hold back the tide.

Anxious to prevent yet another war, Sir William Johnson arranged for new treaty talks to be held at Fort Stanwix, New York, in the autumn of 1768. More than three thousand Natives, most of them from the Six Nations Confederacy, attended the big meeting. Simon and Alexander McKee were two of the principal interpreters.

Johnson persuaded the Iroquois to sell a huge parcel of territory to the Crown. The land that would be opened to settlement included all of present day Kentucky, large parts of West Virginia and Tennessee, and a small corner of Alabama. It was also the prized hunting grounds of the Delawares and the Shawnees.

Delaware and Shawnee chiefs were furious when they learned that the Iroquois had sold their lands out from under them. The Six Nations' response was that the Delawares and Shawnees were subject tribes of the Iroquois, and therefore had no say in the matter. They warned that if the Shawnees and Delawares made trouble, Iroquois warriors would fight alongside the whites.

A scent of intrigue hung over the land sale. By throwing open Delaware and Shawnee territory, the Six Nations channeled the flow of settlers away from their own homelands. In all likelihood, Simon and Guyasuta conferred on how Simon could most effectively use his position to the Iroquois' advantage.

A year later, a delegation of angry Shawnee chiefs travelled to Pittsburgh to confront Iroquois leaders. McKee represented the British Indian Department, and Simon was the principal interpreter in the delicate negotiations. The meetings resolved nothing, but they enhanced Simon's reputation as a skilled intermediary and interpreter. Colonial authorities and Native leaders alike saw him as reliable and trustworthy.

Simon was, in fact, a rarity in that he could live comfortably with one foot in the white man's world and the other in the Native world. He was permitted to sit on Native councils, a privilege given no other white man. This made him the best man McKee could possibly have for diplomatic missions among the tribes. Native leaders knew that if they gave Simon a message, McKee would receive it exactly as they had said it. In 1772 and 1774, when Guyasuta was obliged to travel to the Mohawk Valley in New York to confer with Sir William Johnson at his estate, Johnson Hall, Simon was his escort.

While the Shawnees and Delawares smouldered with resentment over the sale of their lands, trouble of another sort flared up. Even though the western lands had been tentatively attached to Canada, Virginia and Pennsylvania both laid claims to them, and to Pittsburgh in particular. There was a lot of money to be made in land speculation, and influential men on both sides of the dispute would go to any length, including violence, to further their own ends.

Guyasuta believed that if the contested territory became attached to Virginia, the flow of settlers would go south, away from the Seneca lands to the north. Simon therefore sided with the Virginians. The British governor of Virginia, John Murray,

Lord Dunmore, sent an armed force to occupy Pittsburg late in 1773. He renamed the town Fort Dunmore in his own honour.

The local population was sharply divided between the Virginia and Pennsylvania factions. There were several altercations in which Simon participated as a pro-Virginia ruffian. He was quite capable of handling himself him a brawl, but Simon was not a thug. In one incident, when he saw a man about to strike a woman on the head with the barrel of a rifle, Simon deflected the blow with his hand.

Combined with the uneasy Native situation, this intercolonial conflict had the potential to be explosive. McKee worked desperately to preserve the peace, often sending Simon to speak at tribal councils. But Lord Dunmore wanted an "Indian War" that he could use to solidify Virginia's claims. An atrocity at the mouth of Yellow Creek on the Ohio River was the spark that touched off the conflict known as Dunmore's War.

On April 30, 1774, a Mingo chief named Logan, who had been friendly with the whites, was away hunting. A group of Virginia frontiersmen led by Daniel Greathouse attacked his village and massacred two dozen men, women, and children. Among the dead were members of Logan's family.

Even though influential Native leaders like Guyasuta tried to negotiate a peaceful resolution, Logan was determined to get revenge. He swore he would take ten white scalps for every slain Mingo. Joining his raiding parties of Mingo warriors were Shawnees who welcomed the opportunity go on the warpath against the unwelcome settlers.

Throughout the summer and early autumn of 1774, the frontier was aflame as Logan's warriors swept down on settlements, killing and taking captives. Everywhere, frontiersmen were called to join their militia units. At Fort Dunmore, Lord Dunmore assembled an army and then led his men into the wilderness to hunt down Logan. Simon was Dunmore's chief scout.

The Battle of Point Pleasant, in what is now West Virginia, took place on October 10, 1774. It was the only major engagement of Dunmore's War. Logan was not present, and the Natives were led by the Shawnee Chief Cornstalk. The fighting lasted all day before the Natives finally withdrew. One of the Shawnee warriors killed in the fight was Pucksinwah, father of a boy named Tecumseh. With Dunmore's army now poised to strike at the Shawnee towns, Cornstalk sent a message that he wished to make peace. Simon carried back Dunmore's response, requesting Cornstalk and other chiefs meet him for peace talks at a place called Camp Charlotte, near the main Shawnee town of Chillicothe. Cornstalk and his colleagues kept the appointment, but Logan was not with them. The Mingo leader refused to discuss surrender.

That posed a problem for both Cornstalk and Dunmore. The Shawnee chief was afraid that if the Mingoes continued to raid, the whites would attack Chillicothe. Dunmore couldn't claim to have won the war without Logan's presence at the talks. He assigned Simon the task of bringing Logan to Camp Charlotte.

It was a difficult and dangerous undertaking. First, Simon would have to find Logan. No one knew exactly where the Mingo band was camped. Simon was personally acquainted with Logan, and was sure that if they met face to face he would be willing to talk. But Simon would have to travel through enemy territory, and there was a great danger that he would encounter Mingo warriors who wouldn't hesitate to shoot a white man on sight. Once Simon reached Logan, he would have to use all of his diplomatic skills to persuade him to give up the fight.

About a week after the Battle of Point Pleasant, Simon set off on one of the most important missions he had yet undertaken. He was accompanied by two frontiersmen he could rely on in case of trouble. After two days of probing the wilderness trails, expecting an ambush at any moment, Simon found Logan's camp on Congo Creek. Logan recognized him, and the three frontiersmen were allowed to enter the camp unharmed.

What exactly was said between Logan and Simon was not recorded. Logan still refused to go to Camp Charlotte, but Simon must have been persuasive, because Logan agreed to make peace. He entrusted to Simon a carefully worded message to take back to Dunmore. Logan spoke fluent English, so Simon didn't have to translate. He had only to memorize a speech that would become famous for its eloquence and pathos.

> I appeal to any white man to say if he ever entered Logan's cabin hungry, and I gave him not meat; if he ever came cold and naked, and I gave him not clothing. During the course of the last long and bloody war, Logan remained idle in his tent, an advocate for peace. Nay, such was my love for the whites, that those of my own country pointed at me as they passed, and said, 'Logan is the friend of the white man.' I had even thought to live with you, but for the injuries of one man. Colonel Cresap the last spring, in cold blood, and unprovoked, cut off all the relatives of Logan; not sparing even my women and children. There runs not a drop of my blood in the veins of any human creature. This called on me for revenge. I have sought it.

I have killed many. I have fully glutted my vengeance. For my country, I rejoice at the beams
of peace. Yet, do not harbour the thought that
mine is the joy of fear. Logan never felt fear. He
will not turn on his heel to save his life. Who is
there to mourn for Logan? Not one.

Logan mistakenly named a militia officer named Michael
Cresap as the murderer of his family, instead of the real culprit,
Daniel Greathouse. Simon was quite likely unaware of the error,
but he did know that back in Camp Charlotte, the most important
men on the frontier — white and Native — were anxiously waiting
to hear whether or not the fighting was finished.

Simon and his companions hurried back to Camp Charlotte.
When they arrived, before Simon could see Dunmore, he was
pulled aside by a militia officer named John Gibson. Simon
knew Gibson well. He had been married to Logan's daughter,
one of the victims of the massacre. Ironically, Gibson was with
the army that was pursuing his father-in-law for avenging his
wife's murder.

Gibson asked Simon to deliver Logan's message. Simon
repeated it word for word, and Gibson wrote it down and took it
to Dunmore. Dunmore looked over the transcription, and then
told Gibson to read it aloud to the waiting crowd. Gibson did. In
time he, and not Simon Girty, would be credited with bringing
Logan's words to the world.

While Simon was with Dunmore's army, he met a nineteen-
year-old frontiersman who went by the name of Simon Butler. His
real name was Simon Kenton; he was using an alias because he
mistakenly believed he had killed a man in a fight and was wanted
for murder. In spite of the difference in their ages — Simon Girty

was thirty-three at the time — the two men took an instant liking to each other. Young Kenton had heard of Girty, whose reputation as a woodsman and interpreter was widespread. Though he was not yet twenty, Kenton had already had an adventurous life, and had joined Dunmore's army as a scout. He was a skilled woodsman, and showed courage in the face of danger; both qualities that Girty admired. Kenton was, in fact, one of the men Simon had asked to accompany him on the mission to find Logan. With Dunmore's War successfully concluded, the two Simons joined in the celebrations in Camp Charlotte. They had no inkling that earth-shaking events would soon put them on opposite sides in a much larger conflict.

5

Rebellion

Trouble had been brewing between the Thirteen Colonies and the British government for a long time. In order to defray some of the huge cost of defending the colonies from the French and their Native allies during the Seven Years' War, the British attempted to levy a series of taxes on the colonists. Colonial leaders like Thomas Jefferson and Patrick Henry thundered against "taxation without representation," and cleverly made public rallying cries out of words like "freedom" and "liberty." The billeting of British troops in private homes was one of many unpopular and short-sighted policies that fueled colonial anger toward the mother country. But for the aristocracy of Colonial America — wealthy landowners like Jefferson, Henry, and George Washington — there was no greater affront to their concept of liberty than the King's Proclamation. It barred them from acquiring Native lands beyond the Appalachian Mountains, and profiting from land speculation.

At the time that the first shots of the American Revolution were fired at Lexington and Concord, Massachusetts, on April 19, 1775, only about a third of the population of the Thirteen Colonies supported independence. Roughly the same number declared themselves loyal subjects of King George III. In a conflict that was essentially an English civil war, each of these groups denounced the other as traitors. The other third of the population sat on the fence, refusing to support either side until they could determine which way the winds of fortune were likely to blow. Nowhere was the situation more chaotic than in the West.

Fort Dunmore was divided between Patriots and Loyalists; between merchants who wanted to keep the fur trade in business, and speculators who were anxious to open the land to settlers. Many people felt their allegiances being pulled in more than one direction. Lord Dunmore prepared a secret list of men he considered true subjects of the king, who could be depended upon in case of trouble. One of the names was that of Simon Girty of the Virginia militia, who had recently been promoted to lieutenant. But Dunmore was soon obliged to leave for the east. His militia was disbanded, and Fort Dunmore became Pittsburgh again. Simon was left without a commission and under a cloud of mistrust as to where his loyalties lay. The Continental Congress appointed a Pennsylvania merchant named Richard Butler as the American Indian Agent for Pittsburgh. Butler hated Natives, "Injun lovers," and anyone who had been associated with Dunmore. That made Simon doubly suspect, as far as Butler was concerned.

Military leaders on both sides wanted the Natives as allies. Most Native leaders believed it would be in their best interests to fight for the British, but they worried about what the consequences would be if the rebels won. Some, like Guyasuta, favoured neutrality. If the Natives stayed out of the white man's war, they reasoned, then no one would have any cause to be angry with them when it was over, and they could resume trading with the winner. But the very ground upon which the Natives lived was central to the causes of the conflict, and remaining neutral would be next to impossible.

In the midst of this confusing situation, Simon went back to work for McKee, a staunch Loyalist. There were still issues with the Mingoes and the Delawares that McKee, as the representative of the British Indian Department, had to settle, and Simon's assistance was invaluable. But Simon also listened to the arguments of George Morgan, who believed that even with independence from the Crown, whites and Natives could live in harmony and have a strong, profitable fur trade.

Simon was particularly concerned about the situation of the Six Nations. The Mohawks had firmly allied themselves with the British, but the other five tribes favoured neutrality. However, if they should follow the Mohawk lead, and he joined the rebels, would he actually go to war against his Iroquois brothers?

Meanwhile, Simon was in demand as an interpreter. Early in July of 1775, a delegation from the Six Nations insisted that Simon translate in all matters between them and whoever was in charge of Pittsburgh. Later that month, commissioners from the Virginia Assembly asked Simon to be guide and interpreter for Captain James Woods, who was being sent among the tribes on an important diplomatic mission. Even though some leaders, George Washington among them, wanted to recruit the Natives as allies, others like Benjamin Franklin and Patrick Henry felt they would have a better chance of just persuading the tribes to keep out of the war. Captain Wood's assignment was to carry their message of friendship to the Natives and invite the chiefs to a peace conference at Pittsburgh.

Simon accepted the job. He was being paid to be an interpreter, guide, and bodyguard. He would not be doing any negotiating. This would give him an opportunity to move among the different tribes and get some idea about where they stood concerning the escalating conflict.

Simon and Wood set out from Pittsburgh on July 18. The mission proved to be much more dangerous than either man had anticipated. British agents from Detroit had already been through the country. They had urged the warriors to join the British in the fight against the Long Knives, who, they warned, wanted nothing more than to steal their lands. Everywhere they visited, the British left the Natives with gifts of rum — plenty of it!

The Delawares received Simon and Wood hospitably, but elsewhere they encountered drunken warriors who regarded them with suspicion and even anger. The Mingoes and Shawnees were particularly hostile. It was up to Wood to do the talking, through Simon, but it was Simon's knowledge of Native protocol, and the fact that he knew many of the chiefs personally, that allowed Wood the chance to speak in the first place. Even that was not always a guarantee of safety.

One night Simon and Wood were asleep in their camp outside Logan's village when they were kicked awake by a party of warriors. The assailants shouted insults and threats. Simon knew that the warriors were trying to goad them into a fight, in which they would surely be killed. He and Wood kept their composure, and the frustrated warriors stalked off. Soon after, a woman came to their camp to warn them that the warriors intended to return before dawn to murder them. Simon and Wood hid in the forest until morning. Then they boldly entered the village to deliver Wood's message to Logan.

Everywhere Simon and Wood went, they encountered the same concern: that if the British were defeated, the Long Knives would drive the Natives from their homelands. Through Simon, Wood assured the chiefs that the British lied. He promised that the tribes would keep their lands forever, if they would just stay out of the war. Having completed their mission, the two men arrived back in Pittsburgh on August 11.

Unknown to Simon, speculators and surveyors were busy making plans for lands that had been off-limits to them under the King's Proclamation. Shares were set aside for several members of the Continental Congress, including Patrick Henry. While Simon had been helping Wood deliver the promise to the Natives that the Long Knives had no designs on their country, the promise was already being broken. Morgan, who had convinced Simon of the Patriots' good will toward the Natives, was deeply involved with the speculators.

From October 7 to 19, representatives of the Senecas, Delawares, Ottawas, Shawnees, Mingoes, and Wyandots met in Pittsburgh with the commissioners from the Continental Congress. Guyasuta was their main spokesman, with Simon interpreting. The representatives of the "United American States" made it clear that if the Natives stayed neutral, once the British were defeated the Ohio River would be the boundary between white and Native lands. The chiefs returned to their homes to discuss matters at their councils. John Gibson travelled from village to village with a "Congress Peace Belt": a six-foot-long, half-foot-wide, white wampum belt that was meant to help convince the chiefs to accept an agreement that Congress had no intention of honouring.

By this time the Virginia militia had garrisoned Pittsburgh, making it a rebel town. Suspected Loyalists like McKee were lying low. There were rumours that McKee's house was the site of secret Loyalist meetings. In February of 1776, American agents intercepted a letter to McKee from Colonel John Butler, the

Illustration courtesy of Timothy Truman.

Simon has the appearance of a formidable frontiersman in Timothy Truman's 1989 graphic novel, Wilderness.

British commander in Niagara. As a result, McKee was placed under virtual house arrest.

Simon had been McKee's friend since the day Guyasuta had brought him in from the Seneca country. He had not forgotten how, when other whites had scorned him as "Injun Girty," McKee had treated him well. Now, like an honourable Seneca, Simon did not turn his back on a friend in trouble and he often visited McKee. That did not sit well with men in Pittsburgh who still had doubts about Simon's loyalties.

Nonetheless, the rebel leaders in Pittsburgh desperately needed the talents of a man like Simon if they wanted to keep the Natives out of the war. That April, Congress appointed Morgan as Commissioner for Indian Affairs in the newly created Middle District, which included Pittsburgh. Morgan immediately hired Simon as a special agent. Among his various duties, Simon was to prevent any trouble from occurring between visiting Natives and the residents of Pittsburgh. Simon was still unaware of Morgan's involvement with speculators.

On May 15, Morgan sent Simon on a major diplomatic mission. He was to carry the Great Peace Belt of the United Colonies to Onondaga, New York, where the Six Nations held their annual Grand Council. As the official ambassador of the United Colonies, Simon was expected to convince the powerful Iroquois Confederacy to remain neutral. It seemed an almost impossible task. The Mohawks were already in the fight, raiding for the British. Warriors from some of the other Confederacy nations had followed them.

A month later, in June 1776, Simon stood up in the Grand Council — where the Mohawks were conspicuously absent — and faced the chiefs and sachems. Using all his oratorical powers, he delivered the message that had been entrusted to him. The

Native leaders listened, because he was a man they knew and respected. When Simon had finished speaking, he presented the Council with the peace belt.

Simon's mission was a resounding success. The Grand Council decided that the Iroquois Confederacy — with the exception of the absent Mohawks — would remain neutral. Moreover, they would send Kayingwaurto, the principal war chief of the eastern Senecas, to Niagara to bring back any non-Mohawk Six Nations warriors who had joined Colonel Butler's forces. The Council further enhanced Simon's success by giving him a message to carry to all the tribes that were allies or subjects of the Six Nations:

> Brothers and Nephews: We desire you to sit still
> and preserve the peace and Friendship with all
> your Neighbours. Remain firm and united with
> each other so as to be like one Man. We desire
> you to be strong and keep your Country in Peace.

Simon arrived back in Pittsburgh with the extraordinary news on July 1. Three days later the Continental Congress adopted the Declaration of Independence. The signatories of that historic document did not realize it, but Simon Girty had just presented them with a key advantage in their fight for independence. With most of the Native tribes committed to neutrality, the Patriots could concentrate on fighting British armies in the east and not have to worry about a major theatre of war on the Western frontier. But that advantage rested on the promise of the Ohio River as a permanent boundary.

On July 6, Delaware, Shawnee, and Iroquois representatives arrived at Pittsburgh to meet Morgan and confirm their neutrality.

Simon had exceeded expectations. Then suddenly, on August 1, Morgan fired Simon. The only reason Morgan recorded was that he had "discharged Girty for ill-behaviour." He left no documentation as to just what the "ill-behaviour" was. Something much more serious than a drunken dispute must have occurred for Morgan to dismiss a man he had known for ten years, and whom he had so recently entrusted with a mission of vital importance. Could it have been that Simon learned about Morgan's connection with speculators and confronted him on the matter?

Many of the Natives who had so recently resolved to stay out of the war were having second thoughts about whether the Americans could be trusted. Perhaps they had heard about surveyors on their side of the Ohio River. Warriors of the Six Nations began to listen to the passionate words of the Mohawk Chief Joseph Brant, who was against any peace treaty with the Long Knives. Brant's sister Molly had been the mistress of Sir William Johnson, who had died in the summer of 1774. Johnson had raised Brant and provided him with an education. Brant had seen enough of the white man's world to believe that an independent United States would never be content with the Ohio River as a boundary.

If Simon had in fact learned of the speculators and their schemes, he must have thought that Congress would live up to its agreement and would keep such men out of the lands across the Ohio. He went to work recruiting a militia company, with the promise that once he had 150 men, he would be made captain and placed in command. However, when Simon filled his quota, he was given the rank of lieutenant, while the captaincy went to someone else. Simon accepted this, but he felt slighted. Then, when his company was sent off to fight at Charleston, Simon was left in Pittsburgh on garrison duty. Disgusted, he resigned his commission.

Meanwhile, Morgan had sent Matthew Elliott to visit the tribes, distribute gifts, and try to gauge the mood of the Natives. Elliott reported back that, in his opinion, the Natives were leaning more and more toward siding with the British. Morgan requested that Congress send soldiers and a ranking officer to Pittsburgh. Congress responded by sending General Edward Hand, an officer who had proven himself in battle against the British, but who had no experience at wilderness warfare. Hand brought along a few officers, but no troops. The defense of the western frontier would rely on militia.

As a former officer in the British army, Hand had been stationed at Fort Pitt about a decade earlier and had known Simon. Now he hired him as an interpreter and scout. However, Pittsburgh was soon shaken by rumours of a Loyalist plot to murder the Patriots and seize the town for the British. Among those named as suspected conspirators were Alexander McKee and Simon Girty.

Once again McKee was confined to his home. On General Hand's orders, Simon was arrested and locked in the guardhouse. Girty boasted that no jail could hold him, and to prove his point, he escaped one evening and spent the night sleeping in an orchard. The next morning he cheerfully walked back into Pittsburgh and gave himself up. The unspoken message was that if he really had been involved in any sinister plot, he could easily have fled. A magistrate soon dismissed all of the charges against him.

Even though the fear of Loyalist skullduggery came to naught, fear of the Natives had Pittsburgh in a state of high anxiety. Tension increased as the winter of 1776–1777 gave way to spring. The British in Detroit and Niagara were providing Joseph Brant and his followers with guns and ammunition. Warriors began raiding homesteads up and down the frontier. So many settlers were killed, that 1777 was dubbed "the Year of the Bloody Sevens." As far as most of the whites in the region were concerned, *all* Natives were the enemy.

General Hand wanted to raise a force of at least five hundred militiamen to strike into Native territory. But so many local men had gone east to join George Washington's army that he could barely recruit a company of a hundred volunteers. Hand decided that his next best option was to send Simon to the Senecas to determine once and for all if they intended to fight for the British. If Simon accepted the mission, Hand promised to reward him with the rank of captain in the militia.

Simon arrived at the Seneca town of Connewago, near the Allegheny River, on November 14, 1777. He was allowed to deliver General Hand's enquiry to an assembly. Then he had to wait while the chiefs and sachems deliberated over an answer.

As Simon walked around the town and talked to people, he began to feel something he had not experienced while among the Senecas since he was a boy — a disturbing sense of unease — that somehow he was not welcome. He soon realized that some of the Seneca warriors had already taken up the hatchet against the Americans. He heard stories of raids in which warriors had stolen horses and taken scalps and prisoners. Some captives had been put to death. Suddenly the chilling realization struck Simon that his own life could be in danger. When at last Simon was called to the council house, he found himself face to face with Guyasuta!

For years Guyasuta and Simon had been as close as father and son. Now the aging chief looked upon Simon as an enemy. He told Simon that he didn't trust the enemies of King George. He and the Seneca people believed that the Americans intended to cheat them out of their lands as soon as the British were gone.

In the spring, said Guyasuta, the Senecas and most of their Iroquois brethren would go to war against the Long Knives.

Simon told Guyasuta that the Americans had just won a big victory over the British, capturing General John Burgoyne and his whole army. This news seemed to make no impression on Guyasuta. But what the chief said next was like a knife through Simon's heart.

Guyasuta said that Simon had not come to Connewago as a friend, but as a spy for the Americans. The council had decided to turn him over to the British at Niagara. If Simon accepted the council's decision, he would be free to roam around the camp until it was time to leave for Niagara. Otherwise he would be bound and kept under guard.

For once Simon was speechless, for if he tried to say a word, his voice would betray his emotion. This was the man whose trust and respect meant more to him than that of any other person in the world — telling him that he was no longer considered a Seneca! When Simon was able to speak, he quietly said that he accepted the council's decision. For the first time in his life, Simon had lied to Guyasuta. He couldn't allow them to take him to Niagara. The British would hang him as a spy!

Two days later, pretending that he was going to hunt turkeys, Simon grabbed his rifle, jumped onto his horse, and rode out of Connewago. He raced for the Allegheny River, knowing that soon he would be pursued. That night, at a riverside village, he abandoned his horse and took a canoe. The following morning, as the current carried Simon toward Pittsburgh, a Native on the riverbank hailed him and asked his name. Simon replied, giving a false name.

"You lie!" the warrior cried. "You are Simon Girty! You must come with me."

Simon refused. The warrior shot at him, but he was well out of range. However, the incident confirmed to Simon that the Senecas considered him a fugitive. The irony of it was bitter. In trying to prove his worth to the Americans, most of whom mistrusted him and looked down upon him as "Injun Girty," he had lost the affection of the people he had cared for the most.

Simon arrived in Pittsburgh on November 27. He dutifully reported that the Senecas intended to go to war against the Americans in the spring, but he hoped that once they'd had time to think about General Burgoyne's surrender, they would reconsider. In Connewago Simon had also learned that the British had established a supply base at the mouth of the Cuyahoga River. There they had stockpiled guns, ammunition, and other supplies to be distributed to their Native allies in the spring. This important information was a bonus for General Hand.

His mission completed, Simon went to Squirrel Hill. By this time Thomas and his wife Ann had two children and lived in modest prosperity on their farm. Simon's mother and his half-brother John Turner lived nearby in the old Girty house. James was married to a Shawnee woman and managing a trading post for Morgan in Shawnee country. George was serving as a second lieutenant of militia on a gunboat on the Ohio River. There was little besides everyday chores to occupy Simon at Squirrel Hill, so he had time to do a lot of thinking.

To General Hand, the isolated supply depot at the mouth of the Cuyahoga presented an ideal opportunity to strike the British and Natives at a time and place that they would not expect. The enemy didn't know that he was aware of the post. With most of the Natives spread throughout the woodlands in their winter camps, it would be almost undefended. Moreover, it was only about 160 kilometres from Pittsburgh. To Hand, that seemed easy striking distance.

Hand was still encumbered by a manpower shortage, so he sent a letter to Colonel William Crawford. Crawford was a close friend of George Washington and was involved in land speculation. He had served as an officer under General Braddock and Lord Dunmore, and was acquainted with Simon. General Hand asked Colonel Crawford to bring "as many brave and active lads as are willing to turn out" to Pittsburgh. He planned a winter attack on the British depot. Hand wrote:

> It may not be necessary to assure them, that everything they are able to bring away shall be sold at public venue for the sole benefit of the captors, & the money equally distributed. Tho' I am certain that a sense of the service they will render to their country will operate more strongly than the expectation of gain.

Having appealed to both the avarice and the patriotism of the civilian volunteers, Hand made preparations for a winter expedition while he awaited Crawford. He was thoroughly confident of success. Hand was sure the whole operation could be completed in about two weeks.

On February 8, 1778, five hundred militiamen rode out of Pittsburgh. Only officers like Hand and Crawford wore uniforms. The rank-and-file wore the rough buckskins of frontiersmen or the homespun clothing of farmers. Every man had to bring his own gun. Hand provided powder and ammunition. Each man had to bring his own horse; some brought two, in anticipation of the loot they would haul back to Pittsburgh.

Simon was probably the unhappiest man in the column. His comrades — if indeed he thought of them as such — were all volunteers; they were there because they wanted to be. Simon was there because Hand needed an interpreter, and Simon had no choice but to work for him. He was not an officer of militia; Hand had not made good on his promise of a captaincy. Simon was not even the column's guide. For some reason that was never explained to Simon, Hand had given that duty to a man named William Brady.

The weather was against the men almost from the start. A light snow turned to a cold rain, and the men were soon soaked to the skin and chilled to the bone. Rivers that should have been frozen over flooded their banks and turned low-lying areas into swamps. It took the column days to cover just a few miles.

It quickly became obvious to Simon that Brady didn't know the best route. But nobody asked Simon's advice, so he kept quiet. As the days passed, men began to fall ill from exposure to the cold and wet. The expedition wasn't at all the stroll in the woods Hand had thought it would be.

One morning as the men were breaking camp, Major James Brenton asked Simon to help him find his horse, which had wandered off in the night. Simon agreed and had no trouble following the animal's trail. They caught up with the horse after a couple of hours and then started back to rejoin the column. As they approached the forks of the Beaver River, they heard gunfire. Immediately thinking that the column had encountered the enemy, Simon and Brenton hurried toward the sound of battle.

By the time they caught up with the column, the shooting had stopped. There was no battle, but, to Simon's disgust, there had been senseless bloodshed.

The scouts had led the men to an old Native town that had been abandoned for years. However, signs on the trail indicated that there were people in it. Without reconnoitering, Hand immediately assumed that hostile warriors were using the cabins and ordered an attack.

Excited by the prospect of seeing action at last, the militiamen charged the cluster of cabins more like a mob than a disciplined army, whooping and firing their rifles. They killed an old man and a woman. Another woman and a group of children ran from a cabin and disappeared into the forest. An old woman came out of another cabin with her hands held up. The militiamen fired at her repeatedly. Miraculously, she had only a finger shot off before General Hand and Colonel Crawford put a stop to the shooting. There were no warriors in the town. Hand's only casualty was a man with a wounded arm. The old man had gotten one shot off before he was killed.

The jubilant militiamen ransacked the cabins, looking for plunder. They didn't find much. Meanwhile, General Hand told Simon to interrogate the old woman. Simon spoke to her and didn't like what she told him.

The people General Hand had attacked were Delawares. Of all the tribes on the western frontier, only the Delawares were still trying to remain neutral. The old man the militiamen had killed was the woman's husband, Bull. His brother was Hopocan, whom the whites called Captain Pipe, the principal Delaware chief. The dead woman was Captain Pipe's mother. Bull and Captain Pipe had been friendly to the Americans. Now the women and children who had escaped would carry the news of how the Long Knives had repaid that friendship.

The old woman told Simon that several warriors were camped at a salt lick about forty kilometres away. "Salt lick" was the name given to a natural salt water spring where people boiled down gallons of water to obtain salt. General Hand sent Simon there with a dozen men. They didn't find any warriors. But to Simon's further disgust, two men he sent to scout the area killed and scalped a Native boy who was hunting with a bow and arrow. Back at the column, Hand and Crawford decided to give up on the expedition and return to Pittsburgh. When Simon arrived back in camp, they asked him to take over as guide. He led the men home over a much better route than the way they had come. General Hand's failed expedition was derisively dubbed "The Squaw Campaign."

To Simon's disillusionment, Hand became an object of ridicule, not because his men had wantonly murdered a woman, an old man, and a boy — none of whom were enemies — but because his army had *not* killed even more Natives. Simon finally had to face the reality that he had refused to accept for so long — if the British lost the war, the Americans would seize *all* Native lands. The Natives themselves were disposable, as was evidenced by the killings of the Squaw Campaign. In fact, in Pittsburgh Simon heard a saying which served as justification for the killing of Native children: "Nits make lice." Simon decided that he had placed his allegiance with the wrong side.

6

Renegade

It was no secret that McKee's house was being watched, and that Hand intended to send McKee to Yorktown to be tried for treason. Simon knew that by associating with McKee he drew suspicion to himself, but to Simon that had become a moot point, because the Americans mistrusted him no matter what he did. One March night, a few days after Hand's column had limped back into Pittsburgh, Simon paid McKee a visit. Matthew Elliott was there. The three men had a common purpose: they had to get out of Pittsburgh and make it to the British stronghold at Detroit.

If McKee fled, he would forfeit all of his property, but he couldn't risk standing trial. He knew that in Detroit he would be commissioned as a captain and would have opportunities to regain his losses. Elliott also hoped to recoup losses. Native allies of the British had seized his pack horses and trade goods. He hoped that McKee's influence would help him get financial compensation. He had been to Quebec City, New York and Philadelphia, all of which were in British hands. He thought the rebel cause was doomed, and that he had better go to the winning side. Simon's reasons for going to Detroit were not so mercenary. He wanted to help the British win the war, to prevent the Americans from destroying the Natives.

After Simon, Elliott, and McKee laid their plans, Simon had business to attend to. He paid whatever debts he owed. He signed his share of the family properties over to John Turner Jr. Simon had a room at Duncan's Tavern and Inn, where he stayed whenever he was in Pittsburgh. The landlady, Mrs. Duncan, was a trusted friend. Simon told her he was leaving Pittsburgh because he couldn't work and he wouldn't steal. Then he said, "I'll do all I can to save your family and kin if they should fall into my hands, but as for the rest, I'll make no promises."

On the moonless night of March 28, 1778, seven men quietly left McKee's house unobserved, and rode off into the darkness. They were Simon Girty, Matthew Elliott, and Alexander McKee, who was accompanied by an employee, a relative, and two black slaves. A few hours later a party of soldiers arrived at the house to take McKee to the Pittsburgh guardhouse.

The news that Girty, Elliott, and McKee had fled and were probably heading for Detroit threw the whole frontier into a panic. No three men could be better equipped to help the British cement alliances with the Natives. There was a sudden rash of desertions from militia units. Many frightened families considered abandoning their farms and moving east. General Hand wrote a hasty letter to Colonel Crawford, advising him to postpone a planned military expedition, "as your assistance may be necessary towards preventing the evils that may arise from the information of these runaways."

The "runaways" rode straight to the principal Delaware town of Coshocton. After the murders of Captain Pipe's mother and brother, the Delawares were divided. Captain Pipe called for war against the Long Knives. But another chief, White Eyes, insisted on keeping the peace with the Americans. He was fearful of what the Americans would do to his people if they sided with the British, and the British lost the war.

Simon, McKee, and Elliott were given permission to address the Delaware assembly. All three tried to drive home the same message, but quite likely Simon's oratory was the most stirring. He told the Delawares that the Americans wanted the lands of all the Native peoples, friend and foe alike, and that they should not be deceived by empty American promises. Their only hope, he said, lay in uniting with the other nations and joining the British to drive out the intruders. If they did not, he warned, their country would be lost to them forever. The Delaware leaders listened, discussed all that had been said, and then voted for war.

While Simon was in Coshocton, his brother James arrived. James had been transporting American trade goods that were intended as gifts to help win over the Natives. After talking with Simon, James gave the merchandise to McKee. He had decided to defect to the British side with Simon.

McKee, Elliott, and James decided to move on to the Shawnee country, but Simon wanted to go to Detroit to meet Henry Hamilton, the British military governor, face to face. Once again, Simon was taking a big risk. He was one of the most widely known woodsmen and interpreters on the western frontier, so Hamilton would surely be aware that he had been working for the Americans. Would he be able to convince the governor of his sincerity in wanting to fight for the king, or would Hamilton consider him a spy and have him shot or hanged? McKee gave Simon a letter that vouched for him, but a lot would still depend on how Simon presented himself.

Simon started off for Detroit with a British Indian agent named Edward Hazel and an escort of Wyandot warriors. On the trail they met a war party of Senecas who were also en route to Detroit. The Senecas recognized Simon, and demanded that he be turned over to them as an enemy of their people. In his own defence, Simon argued that the Americans had lied to him and treated him badly, and now he was joining the fight against them. The Wyandots would not turn him over, and the Senecas went on their way. But once again it broke Simon's heart to realize that his former people regarded him with such enmity.

Simon arrived in Detroit around April 20. He was well acquainted with several of the men there. One was Captain William Caldwell, commander of a band of Rangers that had been raiding American territory. Caldwell had served with Simon under Dunmore. The support of men like him, added to McKee's letter, would certainly help Simon earn the governor's trust.

As the administrative centre of a new district of the expanded Province of Quebec, Detroit was a busy outpost of the British Empire. It was a trading centre, a transportation hub, and a military stronghold. Its storehouses were full of the guns, powder, and other materials of war that the British distributed to the Natives. Detroit, along with Niagara, was one of the places the Natives brought their American captives, for which they were paid in merchandise. The British also paid the warriors for the scalps of American men, women, and children. Simon was about to meet the man who was hated in every American home on the frontier as the Hair Buyer!

When Simon was admitted to the log building that served as Governor Hamilton's headquarters, he immediately noticed several sketched portraits of Native chiefs adorning the walls. He recognized some of them as men he knew. The uniformed man seated behind a desk saw that the pictures had caught Simon's attention. "Portraiture is a hobby of mine, Mr. Girty," he said in an Irish accent. "I find the Indians a rather fascinating study."

"They're good likenesses," said Simon. "I've come here to offer my services to the Indian Department."

"Well, you certainly get to the point," said Hamilton. "Please be seated, Mr. Girty, and let's talk about those 'services' that you have so recently been making available to the rebels."

Simon didn't try to hide anything. Yes, he had scouted and interpreted for the rebels. Now he believed he had made a mistake. He had been misled, lied to, and as he saw it, betrayed. He had no doubts that the Americans coveted every bit of the Ohio Valley and beyond, and that if they were victorious they would take it. Simon said that his greatest regret in having worked for rebels was that he was no longer welcome or respected among the Senecas. But he was willing to fight to protect their country from the land-hungry Americans.

To a degree, Hamilton understood Simon's situation. He, too, had been obliged to make some difficult choices. He had received orders to encourage the Natives to raid the American settlements. There was nothing new about that. The French and the British had used Native allies during the Seven Years' War. George Washington had tried, unsuccessfully, to win Natives to the rebel cause — even offering bounties for British scalps.

The purpose of the raids, from a military perspective, was to disrupt agricultural activity on the frontier and deny the rebels of a source of food and livestock. Also, if men were needed in the west to defend their farms and families, they wouldn't be going off to join the rebel armies in the east. But it was the thought of those families that kept Henry Hamilton awake at night.

Sending Native warriors on raids against the settlements meant making war on civilians. Women and children were being killed along with their husbands and fathers. Hamilton repeatedly urged the warriors to bring him prisoners rather than scalps. But nonetheless he was instructed to pay the warriors for American scalps. It didn't matter if the victim was male or female, young or old.

Hamilton knew that the Natives were ruthless in warfare. They were masters of surprise attack and ambush. A warrior might decide on a whim whether to take a captive back to Detroit or sink a tomahawk into his skull. Sometimes it was a simple matter of convenience. Prisoners could be troublesome. They had to be fed and guarded, and sometimes they couldn't keep up on the trail. Moreover, the Natives pointed out that the Long Knives had no qualms about killing women and children.

From his stronghold in Detroit, Hamilton did not see the frightful scenes left behind by Native raiders — the burnt-out cabins, the slaughtered livestock, and the mutilated human remains. But he did see the bloody scalps and the faces of prisoners, their eyes wild with fear — and hatred. Whenever possible, Hamilton sent Indian Department agents with the raiding parties. These were former traders, hunters, and French-Canadian *coureurs* who were to act as advisors and interpreters. They were also expected to try to restrain the Natives from acts of "excessive savagery."

However, the Natives did not consider themselves subordinate to British officers. They were *allies*, and therefore equals. Looking at Simon, Hamilton saw a man whom he knew by reputation to be more than a frontier roughneck. There wasn't a better interpreter of Native languages to be found, the man knew the woodland trails like the back of his hand, and he was held in high esteem by most of the Native leaders. Moreover, he was familiar with many of the rebel commanders and knew how they thought. Of course, he would be expected to kill the enemy in battle, but Simon Girty's influence might very well save the lives of helpless captives.

Hamilton decided that he couldn't afford *not* to give a man of Simon's abilities a chance to redeem himself from past errors and prove his loyalty to the king. If Girty should fail in that regard, Hamilton could divert any embarrassing official responsibility from himself to McKee. The governor enlisted Simon as an agent of the British Indian Department. He would receive a captain's pay of ten shillings a day, though he didn't have an officer's commission. Officially, Simon was an interpreter. But once he took the warpath with raiding parties, he would be, above all, a warrior. At the first opportunity, a great council held at Detroit in mid-June, Hamilton made it clear to the Senecas that Simon had given "satisfying assurances of his fidelity" and was under the protection of the king.

Meanwhile, in Lancaster, Pennsylvania, Alexander McKee, Matthew Elliott, and Simon and James Girty were all officially charged with treason. When none of them appeared for trial, they were convicted *in absentia*. A bounty of $800 was placed on Simon's head. To the Americans, Simon Girty was now an outlaw. If he fell into American hands, he would be executed as a traitor.

Simon's first assignment under Hamilton was to accompany a French-Canadian agent, Captain Guillaume La Mothe, to the St. Lawrence River Valley during the summer of 1778. It was a secret mission, and the details are unknown, but Simon's performance of his duties evidently put to rest any doubts

Hamilton had about his loyalty. In the meantime, James went to Detroit and officially became an agent of the British Indian Department.

Hamilton then sent Simon to the Upper Sandusky towns southwest of the western end of Lake Erie. One of these communities was named after Half King, a Wyandot chief who was a bitter foe of the Americans. Nearby were the Mingo communities of Darby's and New Hell. Early in September, Simon left Upper Sandusky as interpreter and military advisor with a large Wyandott and Mingo war party. Hamilton had also instructed Simon to "attend to the behaviour of the Indians, protect defenceless persons and prevent any insult or barbarity being exercised on the Prisoners."

On the trail south, Simon's party was joined by Shawnees accompanied by James and another agent named John Ward. This large group continued south, and then broke up into small raiding parties of twenty to thirty warriors. The Shawnees headed into Kentucky, while the Wyandotts and Mingoes went to spread terror in Western Pennsylvania. Within a few days the frontier was aflame as the raiders struck one homestead after another. The warriors would attack without warning, shrieking their battle cries. Sometimes the victims had a chance to fight back, often they didn't, and the attack was over in but a few minutes. Many of the warriors carried off captives, but Simon couldn't be everywhere, and just as many victims were killed and scalped. Survivors who managed to avoid capture reported seeing white men with the Natives. Stories spread throughout the American settlements that Simon Girty and other renegades were actually in command of the raiding parties.

* * *

One afternoon in mid-October, Simon, James, Ward, and a Native companion arrived at the main Shawnee town of Wapatomica. With them were a captive woman and her seven children. Simon sensed great excitement in the air. A crowd of warriors gathered around to greet the visitors and look over the captives. They said that people were coming from distant villages to witness the burning of a white man. This was not some poor farmer who had been dragged from his cabin, but a brave Long Knife who had been caught in Kentucky, actually trying to steal Shawnee horses. Everyone was anxious to see the man's courage put to the test of a slow death by fire. Simon asked where the prisoner was, and was directed to the council house.

Simon led his party to the entrance and was immediately invited inside. In the gloomy interior he saw several Shawnee elders sitting around the council fire. In one corner a white man sat on the floor with his head hanging down so his face could not be seen. His wrists were bound and he had clearly been beaten. He was shirtless and his upper body was painted black, which meant that he had been condemned to death by fire. He didn't so much as raise his head to look at the people who entered.

Simon was concerned that the sight of the brutalized man would be frightening to his captives, so he asked that he be taken outside. When the prisoner had been dragged out, the Shawnees wanted to hear all about the raids in which the Girty brothers had participated. They listened with rapt attention as Simon gave a dramatic narrative. Then the elders discussed how the captives should be distributed. Before the prisoners were led away, Simon told them to be strong and not be afraid; the Shawnees would not kill them.

The Long Knife prisoner was brought back into the council house. Now Simon could see that he was tall, blue-eyed, and somewhat familiar, but the man's face was badly swollen from beatings and was painted black. The Shawnees told Simon they'd been unable to question him because he spoke only English. Simon asked permission to interrogate the prisoner himself, and it was granted.

From the moment Simon had heard that the Shawnees intended to burn a prisoner, he had been trying to think of a way to save the man from an agonizing death. He knew that to the Natives, the torture of an enemy was a ritual steeped in their own perceptions of courage and honour. A great warrior would not only endure the suffering, but also challenge his tormenters to do their worst. But to Simon's British employers it was barbaric, and he had instructions to prevent it. Moreover, Simon was still haunted by the memory of his own stepfather's death by torture.

Simon squatted beside the man, who was again seated on the floor, his eyes downcast. He asked a few questions about the number of rebel troops in Kentucky. The prisoner's speech was somewhat impeded by his swollen lips, and his answers were evasive. Then Simon asked him his name. The prisoner replied, "Simon Butler!"

Simon was stunned. Butler! (Girty still didn't know his real name was Kenton). His old friend from the time of Dunmore's War! To the surprise of the watching Shawnees, Simon suddenly embraced the prisoner.

"Why didn't you speak up?" he asked.

Kenton replied, "I didn't know if we was still friends, all things considered. So I thought it best not to be too forward."

Simon stood up and turned to the Shawnee elders. "This man is my friend," he said. "He is like my brother. If ever you were to do a favour for me, you must do this one thing, and spare his life."

Right away there were objections. The Long Knife had been stealing Shawnee horses! He was an enemy of the Shawnees and of the king! People had come from very far to see him burn!

The elders decided to put the prisoner's fate to the vote, but first they gave Simon the opportunity to speak on his behalf. Simon spoke passionately of his friendship for Kenton. He also reminded them that he himself was a good friend of Governor Hamilton, and an agent of the king. Three Shawnee war chiefs took turns speaking, and they angrily demanded that the prisoner be burned. Again Simon stood up and with great eloquence stated his reasons for sparing the prisoner.

Finally, the chief at the head of the circle held up a war club. He passed it to the man sitting next to him. Then he picked up a stick on which he would cut notches to keep a tally of the votes. If a man struck the ground in front of him with the war club, that was a vote for death. But if he simply passed the club on to the next man, that was a vote for clemency.

The two Simons watched with great anticipation as the war club went around the circle. But before it had gone two thirds of the way, they knew that the silver tongue of Simon Girty had won the day. All of the older chiefs voted to spare the prisoner; only three of the younger war chiefs voted for death.

Now the Shawnees heartily welcomed Kenton into the tribe. A woman whose son had been killed on a raid adopted him and named him Great White Wolf. Kenton underwent the ritual of having the whiteness washed out of him, but he was not made to run the gauntlet. The chiefs decided that he had already demonstrated his courage and strength through his brutal ordeal. Under the care of his new "mother" and Simon, Kenton recuperated from his injuries.

During their long hours together, Kenton told Simon all that had happened to him since they'd last met. Still going under the name Butler, Kenton had been a scout for Lieutenant Colonel George Rogers Clark. A brilliant tactician in wilderness warfare, Clark and his Rangers had captured the British posts at Kaskaskia, Cahokia, Prairie du Rocher, St. Phillipe, and Vincennes. These were stunning victories which gave the Americans control of the Illinois country.

After completing his service with Clark, Kenton went to Boonesborough, the Kentucky settlement founded by Daniel Boone. When Kenton arrived, Boone himself had just escaped from captivity among the Shawnees. Boone convinced Kenton to join an expedition he was leading into Shawnee country to spy and perhaps get back some horses the warriors had stolen from the settlements. It was on this mission that Kenton had been captured while trying to make off with seven horses. The Shawnees had beaten him every day, forced him to run several gauntlets, and tied him naked to a horse that dragged him through brush. Once, to humiliate Kenton, a fat woman sat on him. Kenton bit her bare rump, to the great amusement of the warriors.

It did not matter to the two Simons that they had been fighting on opposite sides. Kenton was grateful to Girty for saving his life. Girty would not turn his back on a friend, no matter what the circumstances.

Kenton was up and about within two weeks. Simon took him to a British trading post and bought him clothes, a rifle, and a horse and saddle. Then they went on a two week tour of the nearby Native towns. The friends were welcomed by everyone they met, including McKee, who was running a trading post at a place called McKee's Town. Then, at a Wyandot village called Solomon's Town, their pleasant tour turned deadly.

Photo courtesy of the Detroit Public Library.

This 1794 watercolour shows Detroit as Simon would have known it. It was from here that Simon made his dramatic escape from American soldiers when he swam his horse across the river.

Simon and Kenton were sitting in the shade of an elm tree when a party of Shawnee warriors arrived from Wapatomica. They greeted Simon warmly, but would not shake hands with Kenton. These men had been away on raids and had not been present when the chiefs had voted to spare Kenton. When they returned, they'd been angered to learn that the Long Knife was walking around free. Their leader, Red Pole, told Simon that they had lost many men on the raids, and they wanted to burn Kenton in revenge. They had convinced the council to hold another trial. Red Pole and his party were taking Kenton back to Wapatomica.

Simon translated all that had been said for Kenton, and told him that they had no choice but to return to Wapatomica. Back in the Shawnee council house, Kenton was again put on trial. Red Pole spoke of the wrongs that Long Knives like Kenton had done to the Shawnees, and demanded that he be burned at the stake. Once again, Simon spoke in Kenton's defence, but this time his eloquence failed. The council condemned Kenton to death by torture.

No doubt, Kenton thought there was no hope for him. But Simon quietly said that he wasn't finished. When the chiefs began to debate the best place for the execution, Simon stood up and said that the Long Knife was no ordinary prisoner. He was a brave man, famous among his own people. He should be burned in a place where people of all the tribes could watch and enjoy the spectacle. Simon suggested that Kenton be taken to Upper Sandusky, where all of the tribes allied to the British would be gathering to collect their gifts of guns, ammunition, and trade goods. Red Pole and everyone else took this as a good idea.

The next morning the Shawnees stripped Kenton to the waist and painted his face and upper body black. They tied his hands and put a rope around his neck. The five warriors in his escort were mounted, but Kenton would have to walk the fifty miles to Upper Sandusky. To Kenton's despair, he realized that Simon wasn't leaving Wapatomica with them. However, Simon couldn't appear *too* anxious to accompany the condemned Long Knife. He waited a couple of hours before climbing onto his horse and heading out. He caught up with Red Pole's party about three miles down the trail. As he rode past Kenton, Simon whispered a few words to reassure him.

Their first stop was Solomon's Town, where runners had already brought news that Kenton had been condemned. An angry crowd greeted them. The people were anxious to see the Long Knife's blood. One warrior suddenly ran up and swung an axe at Kenton's head. Kenton swerved to dodge the blow. The blade missed him, but the axe handle struck hard, breaking his arm and collarbone.

While Kenton sank down in pain, the axe-wielding warrior was restrained. After all, the prisoner was not meant for a quick death, but a slow one by fire. Kenton was dragged off and kept under guard. Meanwhile, Simon went to work.

In the morning Red Pole's party hit the trail again. Kenton was in agony from his fractured bones. He was ready to drop when they arrived at the hunting camp of the Mingo Chief Logan. Simon had already paid Logan a visit, so the chief was expecting Kenton.

Logan invited the Shawnees and their prisoner into his lodge and gave them food. Then he had Kenton's broken arm tended to. It was splinted and tied down to avoid further injury. While the Shawnees ate, Logan told Kenton in English that he had sent two of his own warriors ahead to Upper Sandusky to speak on his behalf.

Logan then invited the Shawnees to spend the night in his lodge and to join him and his warriors in a hunt the next day. The Shawnees were anxious to deliver Kenton to Upper Sandusky, but they had accepted Logan's hospitality. By their protocol, to turn down the invitation to go hunting would have been an insult. This strategy, cooked up by Logan and Simon, gave Kenton a desperately needed day of rest. It also bought some time for Simon to save Kenton's life.

The day after the hunting trip, the Shawnees hauled Kenton to a place about halfway between Logan's camp and Upper Sandusky. A large number of warriors had gathered there. Kenton was made to run the gauntlet for their entertainment, then he was told that his ordeal by fire would begin at dawn. Kenton wondered where Simon was. He hadn't seen him since Solomon's Town.

At first light they came for him. As Kenton was being led to the stake, he anxiously looked for Simon in the crowd of whooping, ululating warriors. There was no sign of him. The other end of the rope around Kenton's neck was tied to the stake. Then warriors began lighting the piles of brush that encircled their victim. Kenton was certain he was finished.

Then providence intervened. A sudden rain squall blew in, dousing the fires. The blustery, rainy weather continued the rest of that day, as well as the next, thoroughly soaking all of the brush and firewood. While some of the warriors waited impatiently for clear weather so they could get on with the execution, others feared that the rain was a bad omen.

The third day dawned sunny and clear. The Natives were once again about to tie Kenton to the stake, when a man named Pierre Drouillard arrived on the scene. He was a French-Canadian trader and one of Simon's fellow interpreters who worked for the British Indian Department. He was wearing the striking scarlet uniform of a high ranking British officer, complete with gold trimming. The warriors took him at once as a man of great authority.

Drouillard told the chiefs that he had come from their father, Governor Hamilton in Detroit. The governor, he said, knew that they had captured this Long Knife, and requested that they turn him over to the British temporarily for questioning. He could have valuable information that would be lost if he were killed now. Drouillard offered the Natives one hundred dollars worth of rum and tobacco for the "loan" of the prisoner. He promised that when the governor was finished with the Long Knife, they could have him back to do with as they pleased.

The chiefs quickly agreed to Drouillard's request. Governor Hamilton was the source of their guns and ammunition, and they didn't want to insult him by refusing. Moreover, according to the agreement, Kenton would soon be back in their hands.

They accepted the gift of rum and tobacco, and turned Kenton over to Drouillard to be taken to Detroit.

An English doctor in Detroit examined Kenton, and found that his injured arm had been poorly splinted. It had to be re-broken so it could be set properly. Kenton was well cared for, but he was still a prisoner of war. When he was well enough, he was questioned, and then placed in the custody of a storekeeper who put him to work.

Although there is no record of it, Simon quite likely visited Kenton while he was a prisoner in Detroit. They were still on opposite sides, but Kenton knew that Simon was behind his rescue from the Natives. Kenton was also aware that the Shawnees were waiting for the British to send him back to them. He knew there was no danger of that actually happening, but at the same time he had no intention of remaining in Detroit as a prisoner of war. When an opportunity came, Kenton slipped away from Detroit and made his way back to the American settlements.

7

Traps

On November 5, 1778, an army of 1,300 men led by Brigadier General Lachlan McIntosh, General Hand's replacement, marched out of Fort McIntosh, a newly established post on the Ohio River. They headed north toward the Delaware capital of Coshocton. The Delaware nation was divided, with some of the warriors siding with the British, others with the Americans, and a third faction preferring to remain neutral. General McIntosh had a Delaware guide, but a few days along the trail some militiamen killed him, and the general had to hide the murder from his Delaware allies.

McIntosh had been ordered to build a fort in Delaware country as a show of strength. This would demonstrate to the Delawares that the American army could protect them from tribes allied with the British. It would also be a good base from which the Americans could attack Detroit. Shadowing the army as it marched through the autumn wilderness were Simon and several Mingo and Wyandot warriors. The Americans never suspected that they were being spied upon.

When they reached the Tuscarawas River, the Americans stopped and began to build Fort Laurens. They had a sturdy fortification completed by early December. It was too late in the season to move against Detroit, and food was running low, so McIntosh decided to withdraw to Fort McIntosh until spring. He left a garrison of 150 men under Colonel John Gibson. These men had enough food to last them a month at the most.

All the while, Simon and his warriors had been watching from the trees. Certain that he knew what the Americans were up to, he hurried off to Upper Sandusky to report. He was back again by the end of the first week of January 1779.

On January 19, a Delaware warrior arrived at Fort Laurens with a letter for Colonel Gibson. It was from the Reverend David Zeisberger, one of the Moravian missionaries who were trying to convert the Delawares to Christianity. Zeisberger's letter said that a friendly Delaware chief named John Killbuck had told him that Simon Girty and a company of warriors were on their way to attack Fort Laurens. The information was inaccurate, but it put Gibson on the alert.

Two days later a horse train loaded with food and other supplies arrived. It was escorted by Captain John Clark and fifteen Pennsylvania militiamen. The provisions were a welcome sight to Gibson's half-starved men. The colonel invited Clark and his company to rest overnight at the fort before starting their return journey to Fort McIntosh. That evening Gibson wrote several letters to people in Pittsburgh, which he was sending out with Clark. Simon's name was prominent in the messages. In one letter, Gibson wrote, "I hope, if Mr. Girty comes to pay me a visit, I shall be able to trepan him." (To make a hole in his skull) Gibson thought that Girty was on his way with an attack force. Actually, Simon was camped a short distance away with eight Mingoes.

On the morning of January 22, Captain Clark's company rode out of the fort. Unwisely, they used the same trail they had followed on the way in and they rode single file. Because of the cold, each man had his reins in one hand and his other hand in a pocket for warmth; no one had a gun at the ready. A few hours out of the fort, Captain Clark's company rode into an ambush.

They were passing through a dense thicket when Simon and his men opened fire on them from both sides of the trail. Six militiamen were hit; two of them fell to the ground, dead. Horses plunged and bucked in terror, and one soldier was thrown from his saddle. Clark and the rest of his men spun their horses around and raced for the safety of Fort Laurens. The man who had been thrown from his horse was carrying Colonel Gibson's letters.

Simon was sure that the letters he'd found on the prisoner were important, but he couldn't read them. Simon put a gun to the prisoner's head and told him to read the letters out loud, but the man pleadingly swore that he couldn't read either. Not until the letters were read to him by an English trader at Half King's Town did Simon learn of Zeisberger's warning to Gibson.

Zeisberger and his Moravian colleague John Heckewelder had always claimed that as missionaries they were neutral — their only interest was in converting the heathen Natives. But Simon and other Indian agents had long suspected that the missionaries were spying for the Americans. They had spoken of their concerns to their British superiors, who did nothing. Now Simon had proof.

Simon believed that Zeisberger got the information about an attack on Fort Laurens from Alex McCormick. He was a trader who was often in Upper Sandusky, where he was likely to hear gossip about what the British allies were doing. McCormick also frequented the Delaware villages, and was a good friend of Heckewelder. It was easy for Simon to put two and two together, but he had no proof of McCormick's complicity.

Simon took the captured documents and his American prisoner to Detroit, arriving there on February 4. Governor Hamilton had left with a small force of British troops and Canadian militia, bolstered by a large number of Natives, with Matthew Elliott as scout. He wanted to recapture the posts in the Illinois country that had been taken by George Rogers Clark. The expedition would result in Hamilton's defeat and surrender, and subsequent humiliation at the hands of Americans who despised him as "the Hairbuyer."

Major Richard Berringer Lernoult of the King's 8th Regiment now commanded at Detroit. Simon gave him the documents, and made a detailed report of all he had seen at Fort Laurens. He said he was sure that General McIntosh planned to march on Detroit in the spring.

Simon told the major that even as they spoke, Mingo, Shawnee, Wyandot, and pro-British Delawares were gathering at Sandusky to move on Fort Laurens. They had little chance of capturing the post without artillery, but they could harass the garrison and slaughter their cattle. If a relief column came from Fort McIntosh, they could ambush it. Simon told Lernoult that the chiefs requested British help.

When Simon left Detroit a few days later, he had with him Captain Henry Bird, who was Lernoult's second-in-command, ten volunteer British regulars, and several Canadian militiamen. Captain Bird was officially in command of the party. He had no experience in dealing with Natives. They arrived at Half King's Town at just the wrong time.

Bird was horrified to see that the Natives were torturing an American prisoner. He immediately tried to intercede, offering the chiefs as much as four hundred dollars worth of goods in exchange for the man. But as Simon might well have tried to tell him, once the ritual burning of a captured enemy started, there was almost no chance of stopping it.

Once the unfortunate man was dead, the warriors assembled to hear what the English officer had to say. Simon translated, and they didn't like what they heard. Captain Bird denounced them all as cowards for the brutal execution of the prisoner, and said he wanted nothing more to do with them.

Between seven and eight hundred warriors had been in the town, ready to follow Captain Bird against Fort Laurens. After his scathing admonishment, most of them left. Only 180 were still willing to go against Fort Laurens, and only if Captain Bird was not in command. Exasperated, and with his pride wounded, Bird returned to Detroit. The British regulars and Canadian militiamen stayed with Simon.

The much-reduced company of just over two hundred men followed Simon to Fort Laurens, which they reached on February 22. They completely avoided detection. The garrison's horses had been left outside the walls to graze in the tall grass around the fort. They were hobbled and wore bells so they could easily be found if they wandered off during the night. Under the cover of darkness, a few warriors quietly rounded the horses up and led them into the woods. There they removed the animals' bells.

In the morning, Colonel Gibson sent out a party of nineteen men to gather up the horses and bring in a load of firewood that had already been cut and stacked. As the unsuspecting Americans made their way along the path through the tall grass, concealed

No authentic portrait of Simon Girty is known to exist. This painting by American artist Gary Zaboly is based on written descriptions of Simon made by people who knew him. Note the pirate-style bandana on his head and the silver-plated pistols in his sash.

warriors jingled the horse bells. The Americans followed the sound — straight into a trap.

When the Americans were beyond rifle range of the fort, Simon's men sprang their ambush. It was short and bloody. Seventeen Americans were killed, and two taken prisoner. Sentries on the fort's walls watched as their slain comrades were scalped.

Colonel Gibson didn't know how large a force was out there in the woods. All he and his men could do was watch and wait. Shortly before sunset, they saw a party of warriors in single file cross the top of a knoll about a quarter of a mile away. This party was followed by another, and yet another, until darkness, by which time Gibson's sentries had counted more than eight hundred warriors. They didn't know that when the Natives descended the knoll and were hidden from sight, they were doubling back to cross it again.

During the night, the Natives lit numerous fires, giving the fort's defenders the impression of a big camp; a camp with too many warriors for them to dare attack. The trick worked. Simon had Colonel Gibson convinced that Fort Laurens was besieged by almost a thousand warriors.

Meanwhile, General McIntosh in Pittsburgh had no idea of the trouble at Fort Laurens. Knowing that the garrison would again be running low on supplies, he had sent Major Richard Taylor with an escort of a hundred men to deliver food, clothing and other essentials. McIntosh received the first word that all was not well on March 3, when a Delaware runner from Coshocton told him that Fort Laurens was under siege. Then Major Taylor's supply detail limped back into Pittsburgh. They had been ambushed and forced to turn back before they could reach the fort. As if to confirm the bad tidings, McIntosh received a letter from Heckewelder, informing him that a large enemy force outside Fort Laurens would make it impossible for a relief column to get through. Nonetheless, McIntosh made preparations for another supply train. This one would have an escort of seven hundred men, and he would lead it himself.

The Natives outside Fort Laurens were also running low on food and ammunition, so Simon returned to Detroit for supplies. Quite likely the British soldiers and Canadian militiamen went with him, as he would have needed assistance in transporting the provisions. In his absence, the Natives began to drift back to their villages. The warriors had a tendency to grow weary of siege warfare if it dragged on for very long. Soon, only about eighty of them remained outside Fort Laurens, hoping that they might have a chance to ambush a relief column.

But Colonel Gibson didn't know that. Still shut up in their fort, he and his men thought that any day hundreds of warriors led by the renegade Simon Girty would launch an all-out attack. Their daily rations of meat and flour were so small, they were boiling beef hides and old moccasins.

On March 19 the besieging Natives learned of the approach of General McIntosh's column. Realizing that it was much too big for them to ambush, they quietly slipped away. Three days later McIntosh reached Fort Laurens. The overjoyed garrison fired their guns in the air and rushed out to meet their rescuers. The gunfire and sudden commotion frightened the pack horses so much that they bucked and broke away, scattering their loads. It took two days to round them up, and a lot of supplies were lost. McIntosh had intended on taking the offensive against Upper Sandusky, but without sufficient provisions he had to abandon that plan.

Fort Laurens had been a military disaster for the Americans, even though they tried to claim Colonel Gibson's holding out against the Natives as a "victory." George Washington quickly recalled General McIntosh and replaced him with Colonel Daniel Brodhead. But the name that was getting the most attention was that of Simon Girty, and it was striking fear into American hearts. Of the infamous three who had fled Pittsburgh a year earlier — McKee, Elliott, and Girty — Simon had become the most notorious. He had been singled out in reports by Heckewelder, Zeisberger, Killbuck, Gibson, and McIntosh. As the news of his participation in the siege of Fort Laurens spread across the frontier, the legend of the "White Savage" began in earnest. The Americans allegedly put a bounty on his scalp.

The dread in which the Americans held Simon was revealed during an engagement at Chillicothe in May 1779. A force of 260 Kentuckians led by Colonel John Bowman had the Shawnee defenders trapped in the council house, when some scouts brought news that Simon Girty was coming with a hundred Mingoes. The Americans torched the town and then made a hasty retreat. In fact, Simon wasn't even in the vicinity, and didn't know about the American attack. Meanwhile, Captain Bird, who had gotten over his pique, wrote in a letter to another British officer that Simon was one of the best agents the Indian Department had.

The defeat and capture of Governor Henry Hamilton was a severe blow to British prestige among the Natives, because it indicated that the American rebels were stronger than the chiefs had been led to believe. There was dissension in all of the tribes over whether to continue fighting or make peace with the Americans. Loyalties kept shifting, and it became difficult to know from one day to the next whom one could trust.

Near the end of June, in the midst of this confusion, Simon was sent on a mission right into the heart of enemy territory

— Pittsburgh! He was to collect some documents a Loyalist spy in the community had hidden outside the town. The mission was made doubly dangerous by the fact that Simon could not allow himself to be seen by *anyone* on the trail, because he could not be sure where their loyalties lay.

Simon left Sandusky with eight trusted Mingo warriors. They would have to travel through rough country, avoiding all the main trails. They were expert woodsmen, but there was always the chance of being seen, and they knew what that would mean. The Americans would kill the Mingoes on sight. If Simon survived the fight, he would be executed.

Soon after Simon's departure, the trader Alex McCormick rode into the Moravian mission town of Lichtenau near Coshocton. There, on June 28, he wrote a letter to Colonel Brodhead, and entrusted it to John Heckewelder for delivery. The letter told Brodhead all about Simon's spy mission to Pittsburgh. How McCormick got that information remains a mystery.

Brodhead received the letter a few days later and saw a glorious opportunity to lay a trap for the notorious renegade. He sent a message to Chief John Killbuck at Coshocton, telling him to seize Girty if he should show up there. Then he sent out a squad of veteran frontiersman led by a famous Indian fighter named Samuel Brady. These men were to watch all of the approaches to Pittsburgh, and apprehend Simon — or kill him if necessary.

But no one knew where the documents Simon was after were hidden. Moreover, there were more forest trails leading to Pittsburgh than Brady's men could effectively cover. Would a man as skilled in woodcraft as Simon was even risk using a trail? Like a phantom, Simon slipped through Brady's cordon of lookouts, picked up the papers, and escaped without being seen.

On July 4, he and the Mingoes arrived at Coshocton with an American they had captured along the way.

Simon knew that John Killbuck was pro-American, but two other Delaware chiefs were also in the town: Half King, who was a firm British ally; and Big Cat, whose allegiance to either side was questionable. When Killbuck realized that Simon was in Coshocton, he immediately sent for some of his men — all of them Moravian converts like him — to discuss how they might seize Girty and deliver him to Colonel Brodhead. When Big Cat learned of this, he went to Killbuck and convinced him that such an act could turn the British against the entire Delaware nation.

Half King honoured Simon and his Mingo companions with a feast. Present at the celebration was an American frontiersman named Richard Conner, who was also a Moravian convert. Simon had heard some of the exaggerated stories that described him as a bloodthirsty renegade. He had no doubt that Conner would pass on anything he said to Heckewelder, who would then report it to Brodhead. During the meal, Simon told Conner to tell his brother Americans that he did not wish them to "show him any favour," and he wouldn't show them any. He also said that he and his men had picked up the secret documents and he was anxious to have Alex McCormick read them to him. It was a taunt, which Simon was sure would infuriate Brodhead.

Simon went to Detroit, where he turned over the papers and his prisoner. Then he spent a few weeks enjoying the diversions of the town. He and his brother James drank in the taverns with their friends, and Simon was often a dinner guest of Alexander McKee and his wife. Then, on August 5, a party of ragged fugitives who had escaped from American imprisonment staggered into Detroit. The man who had led them on a grueling five-hundred-mile journey through the wilderness was Simon's brother George!

8

Brothers in Arms

At the time that Simon and James defected to the British, George was a deck officer on the American gunboat *Rattletrap* under Captain James Willing. For two years that vessel had patrolled the lower Mississippi River, attacking British-owned plantations and carrying off supplies. To the British, the raiders were nothing but river pirates.

Then Captain Willing received orders to strip his crew to a minimum and send the extra men to the Illinois country, where they were needed to help garrison the posts George Rogers Clark had captured. George was sent to Kaskaskia. There he was bluntly told that Simon and James were traitors, working for the British in Detroit. George found himself an object of suspicion, ostracized by his former comrades. He decided that his loyalty to his brothers was more important to him than the rebel cause.

George quietly befriended some of the British prisoners of war being held at Kaskaskia. He told them that he knew the trails, was friendly with the Natives, and could speak their languages. If any of the prisoners wanted to make a break for it, he could guide them all the way to Detroit. Sixteen men jumped at the chance, but one of them was an informer.

George was arrested on a charge of treason and thrown into the guardhouse. Fearful of what the result of a trial would be, George escaped. He could have high-tailed it to Detroit, but he was concerned that the other captives would suffer reprisals because of his flight.

George walked fifty miles and then crossed the Mississippi River to St. Louis, which at that time was a Spanish settlement. He stayed about a month, quite likely working so he could obtain such necessities as a gun, ammunition, clothing, and food. Then he headed back for Kaskaskia. On June 19, with George's assistance, four British soldiers, three American deserters, and a Canadian militiaman escaped from the post. George led them on a tough, six-week journey through the wilderness to Detroit.

Once George had been reunited with Simon and James, and news of his exploit spread through the community, he was hailed as a hero. Simon and James took him to meet Major Lernoult, who enlisted him as an agent in the Indian Department. The brothers celebrated by doing the rounds of the taverns.

In mid-September, the British decided that an offensive into Kentucky might discourage the Americans from moving against Detroit. A war party of about fifty Delawares, Wyandots, and Mingoes set out from Upper Sandusky. With them were Simon, George, and Matthew Elliott. They passed through Chillicothe, where eighty Shawnee warriors joined them. A Shawnee named Chiksika brought along his brother, who was not quite twelve years old. The boy, who had pestered to go until Chiksika gave in, was called Tecumseh.

On October 3, the war party was camped by the Ohio River, near the mouth of the Licking River, when scouts reported three American keelboats slowly working their way upstream. The boats appeared to be heavily loaded, and each carried about twenty soldiers. Because of his service aboard the *Rattletrap*, George had experience in river fighting, and it may well have been he who devised the plan to trap and capture the keelboats.

Colonel David Rogers was the commander of the American flotilla. He had brought two boats upriver from Spanish New Orleans, where American agents had secretly obtained gunpowder, lead, and other provisions. As long-time rivals of the British, the Spanish were happy to assist the American rebels. A third boat had joined Rogers at Fort Nelson, near the Falls of the Ohio. In addition to a company of soldiers, it carried a few civilian passengers and six British prisoners of war who were being sent to Pittsburgh.

Colonel Rogers had not encountered any trouble on the long river voyage. He knew that the supplies he was transporting were vitally important to Pittsburgh, and he expected to deliver them within a few days. But as his boats approached the mouth of the Licking River, he saw something that he didn't think he could ignore.

A canoe overloaded with seven Native warriors was crossing the Ohio just a few hundred yards ahead of the keelboats. The warriors had apparently been caught by surprise, and were desperately trying to reach land. Some of Rogers' men shot at them, but they were out of range. The gunshots seemed to panic the warriors, because they paddled even harder for shore. They reached the riverbank, and then fled into the trees.

Rogers was certain that he had intercepted a small raiding party, and he decided that it was his duty to go after them. He beached his vessels on a sand spit. Leaving a few men to guard the boats, he led the rest of his command into the woods in pursuit. Moments later, the forest rang with the sound of gunfire.

The Girtys and Elliott had divided their force in two. One group opened fire on Rogers and his men, cutting most of them down in their tracks. The other warriors went for the boats. The fighting was furious, but the men guarding two of the boats were quickly overwhelmed. A few desperate soldiers and keelboatmen managed to push the third boat out into the main channel and escape.

The battle lasted only a few minutes. Two warriors had been killed, and a few others wounded. Forty-five Americans were dead, Colonel Rogers among them. Five soldiers were taken prisoner. A woman, two boys, and three black slaves belonging to Rogers were captured but not harmed. Besides the men who had escaped on the keelboat, few of the other men got away. A sergeant managed to hide in the bush, and he eventually made his way home overland. Two or three others dove into the river and were carried downstream. They hid in the woods until they were picked up by other American keelboats. The six British prisoners were in one of the captured boats.

The ambush paid off handsomely: a ton of gunpowder in forty fifty-pound kegs, two tons of bullet lead in bars, bullet molds, two boxes of new flintlock rifles, forty bales of new clothing, numerous kegs of rum, and a variety of other goods. The raiders broke open a chest and found thousands of dollars worth of Spanish silver coins. They decided to carry as much of the loot back to Chillicothe as they could and bury the rest until they could return for it. Before leaving, they stove in the hulls of the keelboats.

One of the prisoners was an elderly man whom Simon knew well, Colonel John Campbell. He had been a fur trader and was one of the surveyors who had helped lay out the town of Pittsburgh. Now he berated Simon and George as traitors. Fortunately for Campbell, Simon liked him and claimed him as his own prisoner. At some point on the trail back to Sandusky, the Girtys, Elliott, the Delawares, and Wyandotts parted company with the Shawnees, who were returning to Chillicothe. The Wyandotts took one of the American prisoners, and he was eventually adopted. The other three captives went with the Shawnees.

They were the unfortunate ones. There was nothing Simon, George, or Elliott could have done for them. The Shawnees wanted revenge for Colonel Bowman's attack on and burning of their town, and they would take it out on these three men. The prisoners were made to run the gauntlet repeatedly. Two of them were then burned at the stake. The third, young Lieutenant Abraham Chapline, impressed the warriors with the courage with which he took the savage beatings. He was adopted.

When the Girtys and Elliott arrived at Detroit to make their report and turn over Colonel Campbell, they found that Major Lernoult had been replaced by Major Arent Schuyler De Peyster. He was delighted with the news of their victory, and wrote of it to General Sir Frederick Haldimand, the British Governor of Canada, whose headquarters were at Niagara.

No sooner did the remains of David Rogers' command reach Pittsburgh, than tales of the ambush swept the frontier. Some stories said that all three Girty brothers were present, although James had actually been raiding elsewhere with other warriors. In some accounts, Simon Girty himself shot Colonel Rogers. American hatred for the Injun Girtys escalated, but of the three Simon was considered the most sinister.

The winter of 1779–1780 was the coldest anyone on the western frontier could remember. The garrison of Pittsburgh felt the loss of the provisions that had been plundered on the river, but there was far greater suffering among the Natives whose homes and cornfields the Americans had destroyed. With snow in the woods lying four feet deep, no war parties would be taking to the trails until spring. The Americans took advantage of the lull to construct several new forts, which they called stations. Native spies brought news of these installations to Upper Sandusky and Wapatica.

Early in March 1780, the Girty brothers and McKee, all of whom had been wintering in the Native towns, went to Detroit to report the American activities to Major De Peyster. It seemed to him that instead of renewing their plans for an assault on Detroit, the rebels were going on the defensive. Meanwhile, representatives from many tribes arrived in Detroit: Shawnees, Miamis, Ottawas, Mingoes, Wyandots, Delawares, Chippewas, and Pottawatomies. They were all concerned about the increasing flow of American settlers into Kentucky, a game-rich hunting ground that all of the tribes shared.

The chiefs told De Peyster that they were willing to join forces to fight the invaders, but only if British soldiers fought alongside them. More than any other

Illustration from De Peyster's book of poetry, Miscellanies by an Officer, published in 1813.

Major Arent Schuyler De Peyster was in command at Detroit at the time that Simon took part in the defeat of Colonel David Rogers.

American, the chiefs feared George Rogers Clark. His skillful and relentless campaigns had made him as much of a boogeyman to the Natives as Simon was to the Americans, and Clark had certainly been a thorn in the side of the British.

De Peyster decided on a two-pronged thrust. A force from Detroit would move against Kentucky. At the same time, a second force would strike into the Illinois country from the British stronghold at Michilimackinac in the Upper Great Lakes region. It would be led by Emanuel Hesse, a fur trader and former militia officer. De Peyster sent the Girtys, Elliott, and McKee to organize the establishment of warrior camps and distribute arms and provisions.

As the snow melted, warriors began to pour into Upper Sandusky, many bringing their families with them. There were feasts, dances, and horse races. British soldiers and Canadian militiamen mixed with Natives in an atmosphere of heightening excitement. This was a gathering of the biggest war party any of those present had ever seen. There were even rumours that the British would provide cannons to smash down the wooden walls of the American forts.

Lieutenant Abraham Chapline, newly adopted by the Shawnees, was at Sandusky along with a fellow captive: sixteen-year-old George Hendricks. They watched with alarm the build-up of an army of warriors. One night late in April, the two young men escaped. They would face certain death by torture if they were caught, but they managed to elude pursuers. On May 19 they reached Fort Nelson, but the officers there did not take their report seriously. It was too early in the year for an Indian attack, they said.

On May 25, the largest British-Native force ever to assemble at Detroit set off for Kentucky. Several hundred warriors were accompanied by 150 British soldiers and Canadian militia. There were artillery crews to handle the six-pounder cannon and the two or three smaller field guns De Peyster had provided. The Natives were pleased with the redcoat soldiers, the Canadians, and the big guns. They were not happy with De Peyster's choice for a commander, Captain Henry Bird. They didn't like him, and had little confidence in him as a leader.

With the whites in sailing vessels and bateaux, and the Natives in their big, birchbark war canoes, the attack force crossed Lake Erie to the mouth of the Maumee River. They followed this stream and the Great Miami to the Ohio River. McKee was waiting for them with another six hundred warriors and a herd of horses.

By this time there was discontent among the Natives in Bird's command. The expedition had bogged down because of incessant rain. Travel was difficult on swollen rivers. The chiefs and Captain Bird disagreed as to what their objectives should be. He wanted to attack the formidable Fort Nelson, which would be the most strategic prize if it could be taken. The chiefs preferred to go after the smaller stations, whose stockade walls would easily fall to the British cannons. The chiefs' discontent would have been even greater if they had known that on May 26, Emanuel Hesse's company had been routed by an alliance led by George Rogers Clark and the commander of the garrison of St. Louis.

When not even McKee could convince the chiefs to see things his way, Bird finally gave in. Their first strike would be at Ruddle's Station on the south fork of the Licking River. It was a typical Kentucky log fort that provided protection from attack by Native warriors, but would not stand up to cannon balls. Captain Isaac Ruddle commanded a garrison of just forty-nine soldiers, but an additional three hundred civilians were crowded inside the post.

Bird was very concerned about what would happen to those civilians when the fort surrendered. He gave instructions to the Girtys, Elliott, and McKee to make it clear to the warriors that they must not harm prisoners. He also wanted the Natives to understand that he didn't want the settlers' cattle slaughtered. Bird intended to use the cattle to feed his men and the prisoners on the way back to Detroit. He said that if the warriors would spare the cattle, they could have all of the captured horses.

By dawn of June 22, McKee had encircled the post with an advance party of two hundred warriors. The inhabitants were still not aware of the danger. McKee told the warriors not to shoot because he hoped to take a prisoner or two so he could get some information. However, when the gate opened and a party of workmen carrying tools for cutting grass came out, some of the younger warriors immediately opened fire. As McKee cursed, the workmen dashed back inside and slammed the gate shut. Riflemen appeared on the walls and there was a general exchange of gunfire. One man in the fort was killed, and a warrior was wounded.

At noon Bird arrived with the main force. Even though it was raining, his gunners were able to fire off two rounds from one of his small cannons. That brought a quick cessation to the gunfire from the fort. When the rain stopped, Bird had the six-pounder wheeled into the defenders' view. Captain Ruddle knew it was hopeless. That gun could blast his fort to splinters. He ran up a white flag.

Captain Bird sent Simon into the fort to talk to Ruddle. He advised an immediate surrender, because if there was any fighting, the warriors might be uncontrollable. Ruddle agreed to surrender on the condition that none of his people would be handed over to the Natives. He wanted all of them to be taken to Detroit.

Simon delivered the message to Bird. Then Bird and McKee entered the fort to talk to Ruddle. Bird agreed in principle to Ruddle's conditions. But he added that the Natives greatly outnumbered his soldiers and militiamen, and he could not force them to obey him.

The officers were still talking when the gates suddenly burst open and hordes of shrieking warriors poured into the compound. The shouts of angry men and the screams of women and children filled the air as warriors rushed around grabbing prisoners. Wives were dragged away from their husbands, and children from their parents. The scene was one of utter mayhem.

There were twice as many warriors as there were people in the fort, so disappointed Natives who had failed to claim captives looked for other plunder. Bird, McKee, and Simon tried to stop them, but to no avail. One warrior tomahawked an American who had been wounded during the shooting. Then a warrior shot a cow. This set off a wholesale slaughter of all the cattle in the fort. In the midst of the chaos, a pregnant young woman suddenly went into labour. In a show of compassion that must have seemed bizarre to the terrified Americans, the warrior who had claimed the woman as a captive took her into a cabin so she could deliver the baby.

By this time James, George, and Elliott had entered the fort. With their help, Simon and McKee managed to restore order. Bird was furious, but he contained his anger when the chiefs came to see him. They were jubilant over the easy victory. Their warriors had hundreds of captives who were being loaded up with booty — everything from clothing to copper kettles. The chiefs were now anxious for Bird and his cannons to go with them to the next target, Martin's Station, just a few miles away.

Captain Bird had learned a valuable lesson the last time he'd lost his temper with his Native allies. This time he calmly told the chiefs of his disappointment in their lack of control over their men. He was displeased with the killing of the wounded man and with the slaughter of the cattle. Beef that would have sustained the soldiers and warriors now had to be left to rot.

Bird gave the chiefs an ultimatum. They had to agree that all captives would be turned over to him. They also had to promise that there would be no further slaughter of livestock. If the chiefs would not accept those terms, he would take his British troops, Canadian militiamen, and his cannons back to Detroit.

The chiefs went off to discuss the terms. The next morning, they turned most of the captives over to Bird. They promised they would restrain their warriors from killing cattle. As a sign of their good faith, they offered Bird a string of wampum. Bird accepted the wampum. He was sure that the few captives still in Native hands could be ransomed at Detroit. Then he gave orders to move on Martin's Station.

On June 28 the warriors and soldiers surrounded the small fort. Bird sent a captive in to tell the commander that he had cannons. The commander surrendered immediately, trusting that Bird would protect his people from the warriors. The chiefs kept their word in allowing Bird to take custody of all of the prisoners, but in their excitement over a second easy victory, the warriors shot all of the cattle. They looted Martin's Station, and then burned it down.

Angry once again over the loss of cattle, Bird ordered his force back to Ruddle's Station. The chiefs wanted to go on to attack Bryan's Station and Lexington, but with almost four hundred prisoners to feed, besides his own soldiers and the Natives, Bird simply did not have enough food to continue the campaign. He had no choice but to begin the journey back to Detroit.

Among the captives in Native custody was a frontiersman named John Hinkson, whom Simon had known for years. Simon and Hinkson had served together in Dunmore's War, and even though they were now technically enemies, Simon knew that Hinkson was in a very dangerous situation. A few years earlier Hinkson had killed a Delaware. If any of the Natives should recognize him, Hinkson would be condemned to the stake, and nobody would be able to save him.

During a break in the march, and on the pretext of it being a joke, Simon exchanged clothes with Hinkson. Then he went to Bird and told him that Hinkson was "very supple and active," and that he should be under the close guard of British soldiers rather than the unreliable Natives. Hinkson was promptly taken into British custody. That night, Hinkson escaped. Simon was suspected of having assisted him in getting away. But nobody dared accuse him to his face and no charges were brought against him.

There were several black slaves among the captives, and they were distributed as part of the plunder. The ones who went to the Natives were adopted. Two were given to Elliott, and one each to McKee and Simon. Elliott and McKee's slaves remained slaves. Simon set his man free. In further contrast to the evil reputation of the Injun Girtys, it was George who complained to Bird that the captives were not getting a fair share of the food rations.

The attack force broke up when it reached the Ohio River. The warriors went to their villages. Simon headed for Upper Sandusky, and George and James for Wapatomica. Bird reached Detroit on August 4. The following day, Natives who still had captives brought them in to be ransomed.

The chiefs thought that the expedition had been a great success. They had destroyed two forts, captured many prisoners, and returned home with loot and horses. But Major De Peyster and other ranking British officers were not pleased. Hesse had failed utterly in his campaign. They had hoped that Bird would capture Fort Nelson. Instead, he had taken two small forts that had practically no military value. They were certain, though, that the Americans would retaliate.

When Clark learned about the capture of Ruddle's and Martin's Stations he immediately made preparations to strike back. On August 5, an American deserter told De Peyster that Clark was on the move with a thousand men and artillery to attack the Shawnees. Soon Shawnee messengers were in Detroit, demanding British help. De Peyster had just received requests from Michilimackinac for reinforcements, and the men who had returned with Captain Bird were exhausted. However, he issued orders for the Girtys, McKee, Elliott, and other agents to assist the Shawnees in any way they could. Simon and McKee would not arrive until the fighting was over, but the others were in the thick of it.

Clark's army, with Simon Kenton serving as scout, arrived at Chillicothe on August 6. The Shawnees had burned the town and abandoned it. The next day the Americans advanced on the town of Piqua, where the Shawnees made a stand. The battle lasted all day and James and George distinguished themselves, but by nightfall the Shawnees had to withdraw. The Americans destroyed the Shawnee cornfields, and then returned to Kentucky. The Natives began to regard Clark as invincible, but the British realized he had failed to act on a golden opportunity to attack Detroit.

When winter came, there was again hunger in the Native villages, and De Peyster didn't have the resources to do much about it, as he wouldn't be getting more supplies until spring. McKee went to Roche de Bout on the Maumee River to construct a storehouse from which those supplies could be distributed. Meanwhile, Simon, James, and George split up and stayed in different Native camps so they could use their hunting skills to help keep people fed.

In Pittsburgh, too, supplies were low and Colonel Brodhead's garrison suffered from inadequate clothing. Brodhead was concerned that if the friendly Delawares realized just how weak his force really was, they might decide to join their brethren who were fighting for the British. He repeatedly sent messages to them, warning them against the "lies" of the British Indian agents. Brodhead also encouraged the Delawares to try to capture Alexander McKee and Simon Girty, and bring them to Pittsburgh, for which the warriors would be well rewarded.

In late January 1781, Simon was staying with the Mingoes when he received a message from De Peyster to go to Half King's Town at Upper Sandusky and spend some time with the Wyandots. The British were concerned that the Wyandots were wavering in their support, and wanted Simon to use his influence to ensure that they remained allies. When the weather permitted, Simon was to go to the Falls of the Ohio and spy on George Rogers Clark.

Simon was heartily welcomed by Half King, who was a longtime friend. A few days later, he and a few warriors set out on snowshoes for Fort Nelson. A small band of Shawnees joined them along the way. By February 20 they were at the Falls of the Ohio.

The spies soon captured three American soldiers who were out hunting. The men were terrified to learn that they were in the hands of the notorious White Savage. Simon played on that fear when he interrogated them. He learned that Clark had been busy in Kentucky and Virginia, obtaining supplies and trying to recruit two thousand men for a major spring offensive. He intended to sweep the frontier clear of Natives as far north as Detroit. There was also to be an assault on Michilimackinac.

Photo courtesy of the Filson Club, Louisville, Kentucky.

George Rogers Clark, shown here in a memorial portrait painted two years after his death. The Natives thought he was invincible because of a series of quick victories over the British.

This information was pure gold, and Simon was sure the captives were too scared to be lying. Leaving a few warriors to keep an eye on Fort Nelson, he and the rest of his men took the prisoners to McKee at Roche de Bout, arriving there on March 1. McKee sent a runner to Detroit with a message urging De Peyster to immediately start rallying the Natives to make a stand against Clark's invasion of their homelands. McKee believed that if Clark could be dealt a resounding defeat, it would be a turning point in the western theatre of the war. McKee realized better than anyone else that the British high command had Simon Girty to thank for robbing Clark of the vital element of surprise.

Simon returned to Sandusky, where Half King asked him to carry a message to Detroit. Simon memorized a speech in which the chief told De Peyster that the Wyandots and Delawares realized that the Americans had been lying to them. They were determined to fight the Long Knives as loyal allies of King George. As proof of his sincerity, Half King gave Simon three strings of wampum to be placed in De Peyster's hands.

When Simon had repeated Half King's speech, De Peyster wrote a reply which he read aloud so Simon could commit it to memory. He was to deliver it to the Wyandots at Sandusky, and the Delawares at Coshocton. With hardly a day's rest, Simon was on his horse again, on the trail to Sandusky.

Simon was aware of the Natives' admiration for spectacle, so when he rode into Upper Sandusky he wore the full dress uniform of a British Indian Department officer. He knew it would draw attention and command immediate respect. He couldn't have foreseen that it would help him save yet another American prisoner.

As Simon approached the council house, there was a sudden commotion. A young captive broke away from his guards and ran toward him, pursued by three warriors. He was crying for help, begging for his life. Simon raised a hand to the warriors, indicating that he wanted to hear what the prisoner had to say. Even if any of the warriors did not know Simon by sight, they stood in awe of the uniform.

Taking Simon for a high ranking British officer, the desperate captive said that he was Henry Baker, age eighteen. Wyandot raiders had captured him and brought him to Sandusky. He'd been placed under guard with nine other American prisoners. Then, over nine days, the other prisoners had been taken one at a time and burned at the stake. The youth had spent nine horrifying days listening to their cries as he awaited his turn. Now he was the only one left. The warriors had been about to burn him when Simon rode in.

Simon took the lad to the council house and made a plea to the chiefs on his behalf. They agreed to send Baker to Detroit for ransom. Then Simon called for a full assembly, so the Wyandots could hear the message he had brought from Major De Peyster. A few days later, he repeated the speech at Coshocton.

> Indians of Coshocton! I have received your speech sent to me by the Half King of Sandusky. It contains three strings, one of them white, and the other two checkered. You say that you want traders to be sent to your village and that you are resolved no more to listen to the Virginians, who have deceived you. It would give me pleasure to receive you again as brothers, both for your own good and for the friendship I bear to the Indians in general.

Simon didn't know that Heckewelder and Zeisberger had secretly informed Colonel Brodhead that the Delawares had decided to fight for the British. A few days after he left Coshocton, Brodhead led three hundred men in a surprise attack on the town. After putting it to the torch, he withdrew to the Tuscarawas River. Brodhead was afraid that the hostile Delawares would retaliate by attacking the Moravian missions, so he tried to convince Heckewelder to vacate the settlements and move his Christian Delawares to Pittsburgh, where they could be protected. Heckewelder refused, arguing that his converts were neutral and not a threat to anybody.

Heckewelder and Zeisberger naively believed that their Christian flock was safe in the middle of a war zone. A letter dictated by Simon for delivery to Major De Peyster describes what happened at Coshocton, and reveals that the Christian Delawares' greatest fear was not of their warring brethren, but the Americans.

 May 4, 1781 Upper Sandusky

> We sent to Coshocton twenty of our men
> [Wyandots] some time ago and they have
> returned with the following news: 20 April,
> Colonel Brodhead, with five hundred men,
> burned the town and killed fifteen men. He
> left six houses on this side of the creek that
> he did not see. He likewise took women and
> children prisoners, and afterward let them
> go. He let four men go that were prisoners
> who showed him a paper that they had from
> Congress. Brodhead told him that it was none

of his fault that their people were killed, but the fault of the militia that would not be under his command. He likewise told them that in seven months he would beat all of the Indians out of this country. In six days from this date, he is to set off for this place [Upper Sandusky] with one thousand men; and Colonel Clark is gone down the Ohio River with one thousand men.

There were one hundred and twenty Wyandots ready to start off with me, until this news came. Your children [Wyandots] will be very glad if you will send those people you promised to their assistance; likewise send the Indians that are about you to assist us. The Christians [Moravian converts] have applied to us to move them off before the rebels come to their town.

I have one hundred and sixty Indians at this place. Their provisions are all gone; and they beg that you will send them some.... I will be much obliged to you, Sir, if you send me a little provisions for myself, as I was obliged to give mine to the Indians.

I am, Sir, your most obedient and humble servant,
Simon Girty
To Major De Peyster, Commanding, Detroit

Upper Sandusky was the gathering place where Simon, McKee, and other agents were trying to put together a Native army. The refugees from Coshocton fled there to join the Wyandots, Shawnees and others. Then, in early May, a Native leader whose name was already legendary strode into Sandusky. Joseph Brant of the Mohawks was not a hereditary sachem, but as a war chief he had gained fame in the brutal fighting in upper New York.

Brant's sister Molly had been the mistress of Sir William Johnson. Thanks to Johnson, Brant had received a formal education. He spoke English as well as several Iroquois languages, and he could read and write. Brant had even been to London, where he'd had an audience with King George III.

When most of the tribes of the Iroquois Confederacy sided with the British, the Americans sent an army into the Mohawk Valley to drive Brant's people out. With their livestock slaughtered and their crops destroyed, the Mohawks fled to the British stronghold at Niagara. From there, Brant led raids against the Americans. He held the official rank of captain in the British army, but to the Americans he was "Monster Brant."

Brant arrived at Sandusky with forty Mohawk warriors and the promise that more would be following. The other chiefs welcomed him with a feast, at which they presented him with a coat beautifully decorated with seven hundred silver brooches. But although the Western chiefs were glad to have the Mohawks as allies, their feelings toward them were not especially warm. The Iroquois had once defeated the Delawares in a war, and had since regarded them as a vassal tribe. The Wyandots were the descendants of the Hurons, whom the Iroquois had driven out of their ancestral home in Canada more than a century earlier. Nor had the chiefs forgotten the high-handed manner in which the Iroquois had used their lands as bargaining chips in their dealings with the whites.

Then there was Joseph Brant himself. The other Native leaders appreciated that he was a great war chief, and the British treated him as an equal. But while the British considered Brant to be civil, well-mannered, and even tempered, the other chiefs found him overbearing and haughty, sometimes to the point of arrogance.

During the summer of 1781, Simon, McKee, and their colleagues worked hard to build a Native army to resist George Rogers Clark's expected invasion. But it was one thing to recruit warriors, and another to get them to stay put while waiting for more to come. Warriors with nothing to do easily became bored. Many of them gambled away the gifts given to them by the agents. Then they drifted away to hunt or go home. By early August, many of the warriors who had arrived at the start of the summer, eager to fight, had left. Brant's forty Mohawks were still there, but the reinforcements he had promised never materialized. Rather than wait for Clark while their Native army withered away to nothing, the leaders at Sandusky decided to go on the offensive and strike at Clark first.

Brant and his Mohawks set out for the Ohio River. With them were George Girty and fifty Muncie, Delaware, Wyandot, and Shawnee warriors. They were also accompanied by several Rangers from the Loyalist company raised by Lieutenant-Colonel John Butler. Simon and McKee intended to follow them when they had raised enough reinforcements. Besides more warriors, they were also expecting another hundred Rangers from Niagara.

The leaders in Sandusky were not aware that Clark was having difficulty recruiting the two thousand men he believed necessary for his campaign. Many of the militiamen on the western frontier had gone east to join George Washington's army in the fight against General Cornwallis. Those who were still in the settlements were reluctant to leave their homes undefended in case of raids. Brodhead, who personally disliked Clark, would not help him with a single soldier. Clark tried to press men into service, but they deserted. Never one to give up, Clark went to the town of Wheeling to see if he could enlist men there. When he had about four hundred, he set off down the Ohio for Fort Nelson.

Clark had been expecting Colonel Archibald Lochry to join him in Wheeling with a hundred militiamen from Western Pennsylvania, but had been too impatient to wait. He left orders for Lochry to catch up with him as soon as he could. Lochry arrived in Wheeling several hours after Clark's departure. He sent a messenger in a fast canoe to catch up with Clark and bring back further orders. Clark instructed Lochry to follow him at once. He said that at a place called Camp Three Island, Lochry would find a large boat with two weeks provisions for his men. The cache would be guarded by Major Charles Cracroft and eight men.

In the early morning of August 18, Clark's flotilla neared the mouth of the Great Miami River. Hiding in the brush along the riverbank were Joseph Brant and George Girty with their warriors and Rangers. They didn't have enough men to risk an attack on Clark, but they were stunned to see that he had not an army of two thousand, but only about four hundred. Brant was furious that Simon and McKee had not yet arrived with reinforcements. He sent runners to urge them to move with all haste if they wanted to catch Clark on the river and annihilate his command before it reached Fort Nelson.

Meanwhile, two of the men guarding the supply boat with Major Cracroft deserted. When after several days Lochry didn't appear, Cracroft and the other six men abandoned their post and headed for Fort Nelson. They ran right into Brant and George, who took them prisoner. Under interrogation the captives revealed that Lochry was coming down the river with about a hundred men. Brant sent another message calling for reinforcements. He said he was going to attack the Americans whether Simon and McKee got there or not.

Lochry reached Camp Three Island and found the unguarded boat. To his disappointment, the supplies did not include ammunition. He sent men ahead to catch up with Clark and bring back powder and lead. Brant's party caught these men, too. Knowing that Lochry would soon appear, Brant began to set up an ambush, apparently from George's plan. Just as they were getting their men into position, another sixty warriors arrived, giving them the advantage in numbers over Lochry. The date was August 25.

At a place about eleven miles south of the mouth of the Great Miami River, George used a trick to lure Lochry's boats ashore. Then warriors in canoes closed in behind them, cutting off any escape. The battle was sharp but brief, as Lochry's men were caught by surprise and overwhelmed. Lochry and thirty-seven others were killed. After the battle, several wounded American prisoners were tomahawked. The rest would be taken to Detroit. Not one of Brant and George's men had been killed.

Two days later, Simon and McKee arrived with three hundred warriors and a hundred Rangers. Leaving a handful of men to escort the prisoners, the combined force went in pursuit of Clark. However, after five days they decided that Clark had too great a lead and they wouldn't be able to catch him before he reached Fort Nelson.

The Natives and Rangers camped and decided to celebrate the victory over Lochry with some liquor they had pillaged from his boats. Brant got drunk and began to brag and take full credit for the victory. The more Brant drank, the louder he boasted. *He* had set the trap; *he* had been the best fighter; *he* had taken the most prisoners!

Simon knew that Native warriors were rarely humble about their feats in battle. Boasting was a way of gaining attention and prestige. Under other circumstances, Simon might have shrugged off Brant's drunken bragging, but Simon had been drinking heavily, too. He found Brant's claims to be solely responsible for the victory increasingly irritating. From what Simon had been told about the battle, George deserved most of the credit. Finally, Simon couldn't take anymore of Brant's crowing. Full of rum and resentment, he looked the Mohawk chief in the face and snarled, "You're a liar!"

All who witnessed it fell suddenly silent. No one said a word as Simon told Brant that it was George, and not he, who had planned the ambush. Simon and Brant glared at each other. Both men were drunk, but drunk or sober, *nobody* could call Joseph Brant a liar to his face! Both men were armed with knives, tomahawks, and pistols. For a long, tense moment it looked as though they might reach for their weapons. Then, to the relief of all, Brant turned his back on Simon and staggered away. But it wasn't over.

Later that night Brant came up on Simon from behind with a sabre in his hand. Before anyone could utter a word of warning, he swung the blade down hard on Simon's head. Simon dropped like a stone. The steel had cut deeply into his skull. Amazingly, Simon was still alive.

A Wyandot medicine man treated the wound as best he could. According to one account, he even picked bone splinters out of the brain. Fearing that he had killed Simon, and with his head swimming from too much liquor, Brant was about to flee from the camp when McKee confronted him and ordered him to stay. "If Girty dies," McKee growled, "I'll have you hung!"

The following morning, after Brant had slept off the effects of the alcohol, he expressed remorse over what he had done. He blamed the incident on his drunkenness. Brant allegedly wept as he begged forgiveness.

But even if Brant's contriteness was genuine, it did Simon no good. He lay in a deep coma, barely clinging to life. He was carried all the way back to Sandusky, where he was placed in the care of medicine men. There is no record explaining why he wasn't taken to Detroit or whether a British doctor was sent to treat him. Meanwhile, De Peyster learned that because of Lochry's defeat, Clark had been forced to abandon his plans for an offensive against the Natives. Brant accidentally cut his own leg with the same sabre he had used on Simon. The wound became infected, and Brant was laid up at Detroit for months. He was officially credited with the victory over Lochry and never spoke to anyone of his drunken assault on Simon Girty.

McKee kept constant vigil over his friend. For a month, Simon slipped in and out of consciousness. No one expected him to live, but if by some miracle he did, his friends feared that the head injury would leave him mentally damaged.

Then in early October, to the surprise of all, Simon began to recover. The healing process was slow, but day by day he became more alert and responsive. By late November he could sit up and talk, and then even walk around the village a little. Brant's sabre had left Simon permanently marked with an ugly scar that reached from his forehead to his left ear. To hide the disfigurement, Simon wore a red bandana. Ironically, that gave him a piratical look that enhanced the American view of him as a bloodthirsty villain.

Because of the head injury, Simon would suffer for the rest of his life from dizzy spells, periods of blurred vision, and severe headaches. Sometimes he sought relief in alcohol. But after months of being an invalid, by January of 1782 Simon felt strong enough to travel to Detroit. There he would be confronted once again with the problem of the Moravian missions. Because of a monumental atrocity in which Simon played no part whatsoever, he would become a central figure in the story of the horrific death of one man.

9

The Fate of Colonel William Crawford

Although Simon had travelled from Sandusky to Detroit, it must have been clear to De Peyster that he was not yet well enough for active duty. A few more months would pass before the major sent him into enemy territory. Simon spent some time at Detroit, visiting friends and recuperating.

The previous September, while Simon lay at death's door, De Peyster had finally ordered the evacuation of the Moravian towns. Under the direction of Half King, with Matthew Elliott as De Peyster's official representative, Wyandot, Delaware, and Shawnee warriors rounded up the residents of Gnadenhutten, Salem, and Schoenbrunn. Heckewelder and Zeisberger protested in vain. They were forced to evacuate along with their converts. The people had to abandon their homes and their crops, and were barely given time to collect their personal belongings. They were taken to a newly constructed village at Sandusky that soon became known as Captives' Town.

De Peyster had forcibly moved the Christian Delawares to get them out of harm's way, but also to put their spying pastors in a place where he could keep an eye on them. However, he did not have the resources to feed so many people. As a result, the Moravians put in a very hard winter. By February, the situation was so desperate that a delegation of the Christians went to Half King and begged permission to return to their settlements and harvest the corn that was still standing in the fields. Out of pity, the chief let them go.

About 120 starving men, women, and children headed out on the snowy trail to the mission towns. Ninety of them went to the main settlement of Gnadenhutten. While they worked in the fields, picking over whatever the animals had left of their frozen corn, elsewhere Native raiders were striking isolated American homesteads. The settlers believed that the raiders were using the Moravian missions as a base. A hundred militiamen gathered at a place called Mingo Bottom, about seventy-five miles down-river from Pittsburgh. Led by Colonel David Williamson, they set off for the missions with vengeance in mind.

In their zeal to convert the Natives to Christianity and "civilize" them, Heckewelder and Zeisberger overlooked the fact that most of the Americans on the western frontier made no distinction between "hostiles" and "friendlies" when it came to the Natives. All they saw were "Injuns" that had to be exterminated.

On the night of March 6, Williamson and his men were in the forest about a mile from Gnadenhutten. They encircled the settlement to prevent anyone from escaping. In the morning they encountered six Moravian men and women in the woods and killed them on the spot. The Natives the militiamen saw working in the frozen cornfield could not be mistaken for raiders. They wore European-style clothing, and in keeping with the rules of their religion they had forsaken wearing any kind of jewellery or ornamentation. Moreover, women and children worked alongside the men.

When the Moravians saw Davidson's militia approaching, they didn't attempt to fight or run. They weren't even alarmed. The Christians had been living in proximity with whites for years without ever having had any trouble. They'd traded with them and given food and shelter to white travellers. Some of the Christians even recognized a few militiamen whom they knew personally.

Davidson told the Moravians that he and his men had come to take them to Pittsburgh, where they would have food, shelter, and protection. They believed him, and willingly handed over the few guns they had for hunting, as well as their knives. Surely the Americans with whom they had always been friendly would treat them better than the British had at Sandusky.

Photo courtesy of the Ohio Historical Society, 977.1H839.

The Gnadenhutten Massacre. American militiamen slaughter Moravian Christian converts in this illustration by William D. Howell. The victims were actually dressed in European clothing.

The militiamen herded the men and older boys into a building and locked them in. The women and children were confined in another building. Then the Americans ransacked the town. It was later asserted that they found property that had been pillaged from settlers' homes, stolen horses, bloodstained clothing, and even scalps.

It was possible, but not likely, that a few of the Moravians had joined fellow Delawares on raids. It was also possible, perhaps even probable, that the Christians had given shelter to war parties. As dedicated pacifists, they would not have been able to turn away armed warriors. Or it could have been that the "evidence" was invented in order to justify what the militia did.

After the easy capture of Gnadenhutten, Williamson sent patrols to the other mission towns. The men who went to Salem returned with a few more Christian Delawares. Those who went to Schoenbrunn found the place deserted. One of the people there had stumbled upon the bodies of the Moravians the militia had murdered in the woods, and hurried back to give the alarm. The Christians at Schoenbrunn hid in the forest, but the captives in Gnadenhutten were doomed.

Outside the community's chapel, the militiamen held a council. Eighteen men were in favour of taking the Moravians to Pittsburgh, as Williamson had promised them. They were shouted down by the majority, who wanted to kill every one of the captives. Some of the men had lost family members in raids. Nothing but revenge would satisfy them.

The few who called for mercy tried to remind the others that the Moravians were inoffensive and that their white pastors had always been helpful to the Americans, but reason could not prevail against hatred. The council condemned the Moravians to death. A few of the dissenting militiamen left the company in disgust. The ones who remained were powerless to do anything to prevent the verdict from being carried out.

The prisoners were told that they had been sentenced to death. In shock and confusion, first they pleaded their innocence, then they begged for time to prepare themselves to meet God. In an act of cold generosity, Williamson granted it.

That night the militiamen heard an unearthly wailing come from the two buildings in which the captives were held. It was a heart-rending mixture of Christian hymns, Delaware death songs, and tearful farewells. But it affected them not a bit!

At daybreak on March 8, the women and girls were dragged out of their prison and raped. Then Williamson's men began a methodical process of mass murder. They tied up prisoners two or three at a time and dragged them into two buildings they called "slaughter houses." A militiaman would bash in the victims' skulls with a big wooden cooper's mallet. When one executioner's arm grew tired, another man would eagerly take over. One man, after killing fourteen people, handed the hammer to another, saying, "My arm fails me, but I think I have done pretty well."

The Moravians did not resist, but a few who tried to make a run for it were shot down. Ninety-six people were murdered in the Moravian Massacre, including those who had been killed in the woods. About thirty-five were children. The militiamen scalped the bodies. Then, with the corpses piled high in the slaughter houses, they burned the mission down. The ground at Gnadenhutten, whose name meant Houses of Grace, was now soaked with the blood of martyrs. The militiamen did not realize that two Delaware boys, one of whom they had scalped and thought was dead, had escaped. Their story would enrage every warrior on the frontier, regardless of which tribe he belonged to. It left the Natives with no doubt of what they could expect if the Americans won the war.

Just outside Pittsburgh, Williamson's men attacked the camps of the few Delawares still friendly to the Americans. A handful of survivors fled to the fort, where Colonel John Gibson, who was temporarily in command, opened the gates and gave them sanctuary. Williamson and his men were furious that Gibson had interfered, and threatened to kill and scalp him.

When news of the massacre eventually reached the cities in the east, people there were shocked at the sheer barbarity of the crime. But on the western frontier, Americans lauded Davidson as a hero. They fully agreed with his claim that he had "taught the savages a lesson." George Washington sent a message warning his officers not to allow themselves to be taken alive by the Natives.

The story of the atrocity still had not reached Sandusky by March 17, when Simon set off with a band of Wyandots on a spy mission. This was his first assignment since Brant's assault. Somewhere along the trail they ambushed a pair of American soldiers, killing one and capturing the other. Simon learned from the prisoner that General William Irving, the new commander in Pittsburgh, planned a spring offensive against Sandusky. Then the soldier told him what Williamson's men had done at Gnadenhutten.

It was shocking news, but Simon wasn't surprised. He'd been saying all along that the Moravians were at risk, and he'd been highly critical of Heckewelder and Zeisberger for not moving them to safety. Simon blamed the tragedy as much on them as he did on Williamson and his butchers. Simon hurried back to Sandusky with his prisoner, and dictated a letter to De Peyster. The part that reported the Gnadenhutten atrocity was brief and to the point.

The Moravians that went from Upper Sandusky
this spring to fetch their corn from the towns
where they lived last summer, are all killed by the
Virginia militia; the number of the dead amounts
to ninety-six men, women and children.

Before Simon had embarked on his spy mission, he'd told
a French-Canadian trader named Francois Le Villier to escort
Heckewelder and Zeisberger to Detroit. When he returned, he
was angered to learn that they were still in Lower Sandusky,
awaiting a boat. Simon got drunk. Then he went to the cabin in
which the missionaries and Le Villier were staying. Heckewelder
wrote a vivid account of the incident; one that portrayed Simon
just the way the Americans liked to picture him.

> ... [Girty] did return, and behaved like a mad-
> man on hearing that we were here, and that our
> conductor [Le Villier] had disobeyed his orders
> ... he flew at the Frenchman, who was in the
> room adjoining ours, most furiously, striking
> at him, and threatening to split his head in two
> for disobeying the orders he had given him. He
> swore the most horrible oaths respecting us, and
> continued in that way until after midnight. His
> oaths were all to the purport that he would never
> leave the house until he had split our heads in
> two with his tomahawk ... I omit the names
> he called us by, and the words he made use of
> while swearing, as also the place he would go to
> if he did not fulfill all which he had sworn that
> he would do to us. He had somewhere procured

liquor, and would, as we were told by those who were near him, at every drink renew his oaths until he fell asleep.

Never before did any of us hear the like oaths, or know anybody to rave like him. He appeared like a host of evil spirits. He would sometimes come up to the bolted door between us and him, threatening to chop it in pieces to get at us. No Indian we had ever seen drunk would have been a match for him. How we should escape the clutches of this white beast in human form no one could foresee. Yet, at the proper time relief was at hand; for, on the morning, at break of day, and while he was still sleeping, two large flat-bottomed boats arrived from Detroit, for the purpose of taking us to that place.

No doubt the intoxicated, cursing, threatening "white beast in human form" scared the daylights out of the two missionaries. But whether their lives were actually in danger is questionable. If Simon had really wanted to chop the door in pieces to get at them, he probably would have. The next morning Simon rode back to Upper Sandusky. There, the man whom Heckewelder had likened to "a host of evil spirits," assured two American captives, fourteen-year-old Thomas Edgerton and seventeen-year-old Christian Fast, that they had nothing to fear and would not be harmed.

By the middle of May, Native spies were coming into Detroit with information of increased American military activity. In response to the chiefs' calls for help, De Peyster sent a hundred members of Butler's Rangers and a small company of Canadian militia to Sandusky. They were commanded by Captain William Caldwell, an Irish-born Loyalist. Simon and the other agents had orders to rally the Natives. Half King's Town was the assembly point.

The American force was gathering at Mingo Bottom, where Colonel David Williamson's men had assembled a few months earlier. General Irvine would not be commanding the expedition, but he sent a message emphasizing that its objective was to "destroy with fire and sword (if practicable) the Indian town and settlement at Sandusky ..." Irvine's letter also instructed the officers to bring in, if possible, "such [individuals] as have deserted to the enemy since the Declaration of Independence." Those individuals, of course, were Alexander McKee, Matthew Elliott, and the three Girty brothers.

By May 24, 480 men had assembled at Mingo Bottom. Many of the participants in the Moravian Massacre were there. Others had been motivated to volunteer because of Davidson's "victory." In fact, the expedition was dubbed the Second Moravian Campaign.

Because it was a militia force, the men had the right to elect their officers. The two candidates for supreme command were the very popular Williamson, and sixty-year-old William Crawford. Colonel Crawford was the veteran officer who had been with Genereal Edward Hand on the disastrous Squaw Campaign. Crawford was by far a more experienced officer than Williamson, and General Irvine let it be known that he preferred Crawford to Williamson. Even so, Crawford won the election by only five votes.

The Americans marched out of Mingo Bottom on May 25. Some of the men felt compelled to immortalize the occasion by peeling the bark from trees and carving messages into the trunks. When the column had passed, warriors who had been watching were curious to see what the white men had done to the trees. They couldn't read the inscriptions themselves, so they used charcoal to copy the messages onto deerskins. Then they hurried back to Sandusky with the unusual documents. There, the messages were read and translated. The warriors were told, in the militiamen's own words, that the Americans intended to show no mercy; they would kill every Indian they encountered, including women and children.

The story of Gnadenhutten had brought in Wyandots, Mingoes, Delawares, Ojibwas, Miamis, Shawnees, and even warriors from the Great Lakes tribes to the north. If any of them still needed motivation to fight, hearing of the militiamen's intentions provided it.

Captain Caldwell was officially the overall commander, with Matthew Elliott as his senior officer. The Natives, however, followed their own chiefs: Half King of the Wyandots, and Captain Pipe and Wingenund of the Delawares. George Girty would fight with the Delawares and Simon with the Wyandots. McKee and James were with the Shawnees.

The defenders abandoned Half King's Town, and established Half King's New Town seven miles down the Sandusky River, where the women and children would have better protection. Captives' Town and a Delaware settlement called Hell Town were also evacuated, so that the Americans would have to penetrate deeply into enemy territory in their search for Natives to kill. This time they would not find meek Christian converts.

Crawford's army made slow progress, covering just a little over sixty miles in four days. On May 28 they camped on the west bank of the Tuscarawas River. Two men on a scouting detail spotted a pair of warriors and fired at them, but the Natives were out of range. They ran off, and the men returned to camp to report. Now Crawford knew that his army had been seen, and they were still a hundred miles from Sandusky. There would be no chance of a surprise attack.

It took another full week's march for the column to reach Hell Town. When he saw the abandoned village, Crawford realized that the Natives were retreating before him and he began to have misgivings. He called his officers together. Williamson, impatient for a fight, wanted to take fifty men and make a lightning strike against the Natives. However, Crawford didn't want to divide his command. In fact, Crawford feared a trap and wanted to turn back. Williamson and the junior officers were entirely against this. They pressed for continuing, until Crawford agreed to advance at least a few more days.

On the morning of June 4 they reached the Sandusky plains, where the grass stood shoulder high. Crawford had a sense of foreboding as they passed through the silent and empty Captives' Town and Half King's Town. At noon they halted by a spring so the men could have lunch. Meanwhile, Crawford sent twenty-four scouts ahead to look for the enemy.

As the scouts followed a trail that passed a wooded area, Wyandots and Delawares suddenly opened fire on them from places of concealment in the grass. The scouts dashed for the protection of the trees, with the warriors in pursuit. A few of the men hurried back to report to Crawford, who was about three miles away.

The Natives and the scouts now engaged in a running fight through the trees. The scouts were on the verge of being overwhelmed when Crawford came charging in with reinforcements and put the warriors to flight. Crawford then ordered his men to take up defensive positions in the trees. More Natives had hurried toward the sound of gunfire, and soon there were enough of them to surround the grove. Then they were reinforced by Caldwell and some of his Rangers. However, as Caldwell was dismounting, he was shot in both legs. With him out of the action, command fell to Matthew Elliott.

For the next few hours sharpshooters on both sides sniped at the foe. Crawford was knocked off his feet when a rifle ball struck his powder horn, but he was not badly hurt. Francois Le Villiers, who was with the Canadian volunteers, died with a bullet through his heart. An American captain, Joseph Bane, was wounded by a bullet allegedly fired by Simon. By sundown the Americans had five dead and nineteen wounded. British-Native casualties were five dead and eleven wounded.

Nightfall reduced the gunfire to a few scattered shots. Each side lit bonfires along their front line to discourage the enemy from sneaking up in the dark. In the cool of the night, a low mist spread over the ground, bringing a macabre atmosphere to the battleground.

Crawford posted pickets around the perimeter of the copse, which was now a defensive position under siege. Within the woods, exhausted militiamen tried to sleep on the damp ground. But they were kept awake by the groans of the wounded and by warriors who harassed them with war cries and gunfire. Although the Americans were about equal in number to the enemy, they were sure that they faced a vastly superior force. In the dead of the night, fifteen deserters managed to slink past their own pickets and through enemy lines.

The shooting resumed at dawn. With each passing hour, the Natives received more reinforcements. Crawford's men were running low on ammunition and water. Williamson wanted to counterattack with a hundred men. Crawford refused permission. The two men quarreled, but Crawford wouldn't change his mind.

Warriors taunted the Americans and deliberately exposed themselves to riflemen. This was a risky trick intended to make the militiamen waste dwindling supplies of ammunition. Elliott was content to patiently wear Crawford's army down in this manner, rather than mount an attack that would result in British and Native casualties. He had the Americans contained with no hope of assistance, while he was expecting another company of Rangers, as well as artillery.

In mid-afternoon, Elliott sent Simon under a white flag to offer the Americans a chance to surrender. Sitting on his mare, and conspicuous in his red bandana, Simon advanced until he was close enough to the American front to be heard. That put him well within rifle range. He called out loudly to Crawford and Davidson that Elliott was willing to parley. Receiving no reply, he repeated the message several times. There was still no answer, so Simon turned his horse around and rode back to his own lines.

More reinforcements bolstered the British-Native cordon. Shortly after sunset on the second day of the siege, the Natives discharged their muskets into the air in a rolling volley that thundered all around the American position. Realizing that the copse would be a death trap if they remained much longer, Crawford ordered a retreat. The Americans hastily buried their dead, and built fires over the graves to disguise them. Then they fashioned horse litters to carry the wounded.

At nine p.m. the Americans made a sudden break from the woods, intending to race for the Ohio River. The move startled warriors along part of the cordon, and they fired their guns. The Americans had successfully broken through the enemy line, but the gunfire threw them into a panic. What had started as an orderly manoeuvre crumbled into a wild, every-man-for-himself flight, with men plunging into the night in all directions. Crawford was furious to learn that some of the wounded had been left behind. He was also concerned about his son-in-law, William Harrison, and his nephew, William Crawford. In the darkness and confusion, he went looking for them.

The Natives were confused too, and ran here and there in the dark, firing their guns and trying to catch fleeing militiamen. Many of the warriors, eager for loot, dashed into the trees to grab what the militiamen had left behind: horses, weapons, packs, clothing, and cooking gear. Any wounded they found were tomahawked.

At daybreak, the pursuit began in earnest. Just how many militiamen were run down and then killed or taken prisoner would never be known. The Americans would later claim a loss of no more than fifty men, but Elliott reported that the Americans had between two hundred and 250 killed or captured. He said he counted more than one hundred bodies in and around the copse of trees alone.

David Williamson and about 250 men found their way to Half King's Old Town. They fought off pursuing warriors, and then ran for home. Williamson escaped Native vengeance, and another man would pay for the crimes of "the hero of Gnadenhutten."

Colonel Crawford didn't join in the headlong flight of his disintegrated army. He stayed behind to search for his missing nephew and son-in-law. He met up with the company's surgeon, Dr. John Knight. For a day and a night the two men managed to avoid warriors who were hunting down American stragglers. Then they were caught by a band of Delawares.

Crawford's uniform gave him away as a high ranking officer, and the Delawares immediately mistook him for Williamson. They hauled him and Knight to one of their villages, beat them, and condemned them to death by fire. In desperation, Crawford begged his captors to allow him to speak to Simon Girty.

It was Crawford's great misfortune to have been captured by the Delawares. Although some American prisoners had been put to death, most of those captured by warriors of other tribes were being sent to Detroit for ransom, thanks largely to the influence of the Girtys, McKee, and Elliott. But the Delawares, whose own people had been the victims at Gnadenhutten, wanted brutal retribution. Moreover, nothing could convince them to show clemency to the man they thought was responsible.

Two days after Crawford's capture, Simon learned that the Delawares had a "Big Captain" whom they intended to burn. He was under the impression that they had seized Williamson. But when he went into the cabin in the Delaware village where the prisoner was being held, he saw that the bruised and dejected-looking man was Crawford, with whom he had been well acquainted before the war.

Girty immediately told the Delawares that their prisoner was not Davidson. They replied that he would burn anyway, but they gave Simon permission to speak to him. Among those who witnessed the conversation were a Moravian convert named Tom Jelloway and a young American captive named Elizabeth Turner.

Crawford asked Simon if he knew anything about his son-in-law and nephew. Simon told him they had both been captured by the Shawnees and would be ransomed. This was a merciful lie. Harrison and young Crawford had indeed been captured by the Shawnees, but both had been put to death at Wapatomica.

Simon told Crawford that he was in an extremely dangerous situation because the Delawares held him responsible for the Moravian massacre. Crawford was stunned. He said that he'd had nothing to do with Gnadenhutten. He pleaded with Simon to convince the Delawares of that. He told Simon that if he were spared, he would divulge important military information.

Simon knew that it would take a miracle for the Delawares to surrender Crawford to the British. He told Crawford that he would do everything in his power to save him, but that his best hope lay in escape. None of the warriors in the cabin spoke English. Simon quietly told Crawford that if he could somehow get loose that night, there would be a man waiting nearby with a horse to take him to Detroit. But Crawford, perhaps because of his pain and exhaustion, seemed unresponsive to that idea and placed greater hope in the influence of Simon and the British officers to save him.

Elliott, as De Peyster's representative, tried to ransom Crawford and failed. McKee wasn't present, but he had received news of Crawford's situation from Simon and Elliott. He tried to use his connections in the colonel's behalf, but to no avail.

The next day, June 11, the Delawares took Crawford to Half King's Old Town, where Dr. Knight and nine other American prisoners were being held. The whole group was started on the trail to Pipe's Town, but along the way the warriors tomahawked and scalped the other nine captives. Then they forced Crawford and Knight to run the gauntlet. The two men were bloodied and bruised by the time they reached Pipe's Town.

A large number of men, women, and children had gathered for the burning. When they saw the captives they jeered and shouted obscenities. Knight was held back while Crawford was dragged before a council of Delaware chiefs that included

Captain Pipe and Wingenund. Elliott was there, wearing his British officer's dress uniform. However, if he'd hoped the scarlet coat would impress the chiefs, he was sorely disappointed. Simon was also present.

The "trial" began with Captain Pipe making an impassioned speech about Crawford leading an army that included Williamson and many of the Long Knives who had murdered the people of Gnadenhutten. He said that the Americans had lied to the Delawares time after time. He reminded the chiefs of Delawares who had been friendly to the Americans, but had nonetheless been slain by them.

After Simon translated all that Captain Pipe had said, Crawford once again denied being at Gnadenhutten. He said that he deplored what Williamson had done, and sincerely regretted that it had happened. Then Crawford asked Simon to remind the chiefs that years earlier he had protected Indians during the Squaw Campaign. He had, in fact, stopped militiamen from shooting a woman named Micheykapeeci, the wife of Captain Pipe's brother, Bull.

Micheykapeeci was present, and was granted permission to speak. Even though what Crawford had said was true, she did not come to his defense. Instead, she accused him of being one of the soldiers who participated in the attack in which her husband and his mother had been killed, and in which she'd had part of a finger shot off. After his sister-in-law had spoken, Captain Pipe condemned Crawford to death by fire. The Delawares roared their approval. The doomed man's face was painted black.

In desperation, Simon tried to accomplish what Elliott had already failed to do — buy Crawford's life. He offered Captain Pipe his prized white mare and all of his own stores of provisions. He got on his knees and pleaded that Crawford was an old friend.

Simon reminded the Delaware chiefs that he had done them many favours, and asked just this one in return.

Captain Pipe replied that if Crawford had been a private soldier Simon's request would be granted, but because he was the commander of an invading army that was determined to kill Indians, he had to die painfully. When Simon attempted to press the argument, Captain Pipe angrily said, "No! If you were to stand in his place, it would not save him."

Now facing a horrific ordeal, Crawford appealed to Chief Wingenund, with whom he had once been on friendly terms. But Wingenund told him, "If Williamson had been taken, you might have been saved, but as it is, no one would dare to interfere on your behalf. The King of England, if he were to come in person, could not save you."

The Delawares dragged Crawford to a place of execution just outside the village. A stake had been erected and fires were burning. Simon made a last, futile plea for Crawford. All out of patience, Captain Pipe told Simon that if he said another word, he would take Crawford's place.

Crawford called out to Simon, asking if the warriors were going to burn him. Simon answered yes. Crawford said that he would take it patiently, looked skyward, and prayed. Then the torture began.

The warriors stripped Crawford naked, beat him mercilessly, and tied him to the stake. He endured almost three hours of excruciating torment. Elliott and Simon could only stand by helplessly and watch. At one point Crawford cried out and begged Simon to shoot him. But if Simon had done that, his own life would have been forfeit, probably by replacing Crawford at the stake. Unable to respond to Crawford's plea, Simon turned away. Crawford's final hours of agony would haunt Simon for the rest of his life.

Dr. Knight witnessed most of the torture. He saw Crawford scalped while still alive. One of the warriors threw the bloody scalp in Knight's face and told him, "That is your great captain." Knight was then taken away and put in Captain Pipe's cabin.

The next day, Knight learned that a single warrior was taking him to the Shawnees. On the way out of the village, they passed the execution site, where Knight saw Crawford's bones lying in the ashes. He was sure the same fate awaited him. Somewhere along the trail Knight seized an opportunity to escape. He bashed his guard over the head with a piece of firewood and then fled. After many days of hard travel through the wilderness, Knight made it to Pittsburgh.

Photo courtesy of the Seneca County Museum, Tiffin, Ohio.

The death of Colonel William Crawford. His body covered with gunpowder burns, Crawford suffered a slow, painful death. Looking on are Simon (on the white horse) and Matthew Elliott (British officer on the left). Dr. John Knight (lower right) later escaped. Although Simon tried to buy Crawford's life, he was seen as a sadistic fiend.

Simon personally reported the details of Crawford's death to Captain Caldwell, telling him that "Crawford died like a hero." Caldwell immediately sent a letter that included Simon's statement to De Peyster. The major was outraged when he read of Crawford's cruel execution. When he heard soon after that the chiefs had vowed to burn every American who fell into their hands, he ordered McKee to tell the Natives that he would refuse them any further assistance if they did not desist from such barbarism. De Peyster placed responsibility for Crawford's terrible fate squarely on the Americans' doorstep. He wrote to Thomas Brown, the Superintendent of Indian Affairs at Detroit:

> Sir — I am happy to inform you that the Indians from this quarter have gained a complete victory over six hundred of the enemy who had penetrated as far as Sandusky, with a view of destroying the Wyandots, men, women, and children, as they had done with ninety-six of the Christian Indians at [Gnadentutten] a few weeks before … Colonel Crawford, who commanded, was taken in the pursuit and put to death by the Delawares, notwithstanding every means had been tried by an Indian officer present, to save his life. This Delawares declare they did in retaliation for the affair of [Gnadenhutten]. I am sorry that the imprudence of the enemy has been the means of reviving the old savage custom of putting their prisoners to death, which, with much pains and expense, we had weaned the Indians from, in this neighborhood....

However, in the American settlements — and eventually in all of the rebelling colonies — blame for Crawford's horrible death, and much more, would fall on the head of one man. David Williamson and other survivors of the Battle of Sandusky had straggled into Pittsburgh with exaggerated accounts of massive British and Native forces that had treacherously ambushed them. But however anyone tried to gloss things over, Sandusky was a humiliating defeat which left the settlements open to further raids. Then Dr. Knight arrived and attention shifted from Crawford's defeat to Crawford's death.

Dr. Knight reported everything he had seen and experienced to General Irvine. Then he was interviewed by a local lawyer and journalist named Hugh Henry Brackenridge. The story that Brackenridge wrote wasn't exactly the same one Knight had told to Irvine.

Brackenridge agreed with the opinion then prevalent among the American frontiersmen and settlers that the Natives were an inferior race; "animals vulgarly styled," as he put it. As far as he was concerned, they were beyond all hope of being "civilized," and should be exterminated. Brackenridge believed he had solid proof of his convictions in the shocking story of Colonel Crawford. More than that, he had a villain! In Simon Girty, Brackenridge saw what to him was the most vile creature that could possibly exist — a white man who had sunk to the level of the degenerate Natives.

In his writings, Brackenridge embellished Dr. Knight's story. He made no mention of the efforts made by Simon or anyone else to save Crawford. Instead, he portrayed Simon as a fiend who mocked the suffering Crawford, and "laughed heartily, and by all his gestures seemed delighted at the horrid scene." Brackenridge's lurid, fictitious version of Dr. Knight's eyewitness account was widely published. It was a sensation, as he'd hoped it would be.

Settlers and the people in the eastern cities had heard chilling stories about Natives torturing prisoners. Now they had a vivid account from a man who had actually *seen* it. And gloating over the victim's agony was the infamous White Savage. Brackenridge's presentation of Dr. Knight's narrative thoroughly demonized the Natives, the British, and especially Simon Girty.

10

Blue Licks

Nine-year-old Jonathan Alder had been a captive in the Shawnee town of Chillicothe for a year when he met Simon. The boy had been adopted, and his Native parents treated him well, but Jonathan was homesick. He didn't know who the strange white man was who sat down with him and asked him how he was being treated and whether he liked living among the Indians. When Jonathan said he wanted to go home, the man identified himself as Simon Girty, and said that he was originally from Pennsylvania.

Simon told Jonathan that if he was truly unhappy living with the Shawnees, he would buy him and take him across the lake to the British, who would teach him a trade. However, he said that Jonathan's chances of getting back home would be better if he stayed with the Natives, because he would likely be exchanged for another prisoner. Moreover, the war would soon be over, and then Jonathan would be free to go where he wished. He might even learn to like living with the Natives and want to stay with them.

Simon said that he would be back in two weeks, and if Jonathan still wanted to leave the Shawnees, he would take him to the British. True to his word, Simon returned two weeks later and asked Jonathan if he had made up his mind. The boy said that he had decided to stay with the Indians. Simon told him that if he was a good boy, someday he would be sure to get back to his folks. Jonathan remained with the Natives for many years, and as an adult fought with them against the Americans.

In July of 1782, Simon and his brothers were at Wapatomica when Captain Caldwell rode in with eighty Rangers. He wanted the Shawnees to join him in attacks on Wheeling and Fort Henry. The Natives were still flushed from their victory at Sandusky, so three hundred Shawnee warriors eagerly joined Caldwell. The Girty brothers joined the expedition, too. However, they were just two days out of Wapatomica when messengers brought the news that George Rogers Clark was about to move on the Shawnee towns with a large body of troops and artillery.

Alarmed, Caldwell sent two Canadians and forty warriors to spy on Clark's army and hurried his men back to Chillicothe. Meanwhile, Major De Peyster received word that General Irvine, anxious to avenge Colonel Crawford, was raising an army at Pittsburgh for another campaign against Sandusky, and perhaps even against Detroit. He sent out another company of Rangers to reinforce Caldwell.

Elliott, McKee, and all three Girty brothers were busy raising a Native army. Shawnees, Wyandots, Delawares, Mingoes, Pottawatamis, Ottawas, Miamis, and Ojibwas assembled at Chillicothe for a big council. They had heard that the British

General Cornwallis had surrendered to Washington at Yorktown, and the war would soon be over. They were afraid that if the British made peace with the Americans, then the Long Knives would turn all of their strength and fury against the tribes. The chiefs had to decide whether or not their warriors could prevent the Americans from taking their lands. McKee, Elliott, and the Girtys argued that they could.

Simon, the most eloquent of the Indian agents, delivered a stirring speech. He listed the wrongs the Americans had done to the Native peoples. He spoke of the value of Kentucky as a hunting ground they all shared, and which at that moment was filling up with settlers who had no right to it. Simon impressed upon the Natives that they had to unite in a war to prevent not only the loss of their homes and way of life, but also save themselves from extinction. When Simon finally finished speaking, his listeners roared their approval and vowed to keep fighting.

Warriors streamed into Chillicothe, still burning with anger over the Moravian Massacre, and encouraged by the victory at Sandusky. Eleven hundred men from the various tribes were ready to take to the warpath. McKee wrote to De Peyster that it was the greatest body of Indians collected in one place since the start of the war.

But the invasion the chiefs had been expecting didn't come. After the disaster at Sandusky, neither Clark nor Irvine could raise enough men for a successful campaign. The warriors became impatient with waiting. In spite of the arguments of Captain Caldwell, Simon, and the other agents, they began to leave Chillicothe for their home villages.

Caldwell, McKee, Elliott, and the Girty brothers decided to take the offensive before the Native army melted away to nothing. With fifty Rangers and three hundred warriors, most of whom were Wyandots, they set out for Kentucky. Their target was a fort called Bryan's Station.

Located a few miles northeast of present day Lexington, Kentucky, Bryan's Station was, for a wooden fort, a formidable stronghold. It had a stout palisade surrounding a compound two hundred yards by fifty yards. The corner blockhouses had gunports from which sharpshooters could cover every approach to the walls and gates. Bryan's Station would be difficult for an attack force without artillery to take, and Caldwell had no cannons. Since he couldn't blast holes in the stockade, he would try trickery.

The warriors and Rangers reached their objective on the night of April 14, 1782. Caldwell had them surround the fort, keeping out of sight and beyond rifle range. His plan was to dupe the defenders into thinking that they were under attack by a much smaller force than what was actually concealed in the woods. If some of the garrison could be lured into a trap, or if enough riflemen could be drawn away from one wall, then Simon could lead the main body of warriors in a rush to set the wall on fire.

For the people in Bryan's Station, dawn came with a crash of gunfire as a hundred Wyandots emerged from the forest southeast of the fort and started shooting. To Caldwell's disappointment, the Americans didn't take the bait. Instead, two riders on fast horses galloped out of the fort to go for help. Caldwell didn't want to reveal his men's positions, so he allowed the horsemen to pass through. He was sure he could take the fort before enemy reinforcements arrived.

Bryan's Station had one main weakness — there was no source of water inside the walls. The inhabitants got their water from a spring a short distance from the front gate. The water supply inside the fort was low, and in the blazing summer heat, the defenders doubted that they could hold out until help came if they didn't replenish it. What happened next was one of the bravest acts in all the years of frontier warfare.

The defenders were certain that the enemy was watching the spring and that any men who tried to get to it would be ambushed. However, some courageous women volunteered to go for water. Acting as calmly as if it were an ordinary summer day, the women went out of the gates, walked past the warriors they knew were hiding in the woods, and filled their buckets at the spring. The warriors could easily have taken them prisoner, but once again, Caldwell didn't want to let the Americans know that he had them surrounded. If his plan worked, they would surrender whether they had water or not.

With their water barrels full, the Americans tried a ruse of their own. Thirteen men made a sortie toward the southeast, where the Wyandots had been seen. They were immediately fired upon, and retreated back to the fort. Meanwhile, thinking that one wall was undefended, Simon and the warriors with him charged forward. They were met by a volley of rifle fire that drove most of them back into the trees. However, a few managed to get right up to the wall and set it ablaze with torches. Fortunately for the defenders, a favourable wind kept the flames from doing much damage.

Now Caldwell became concerned that assistance would be on the way. He ordered Simon to take some of the warriors and set up an ambush. Before long, a company of about thirty men appeared, half of them mounted. When they came within range, Simon's men opened fire. None of the horsemen were hit. They galloped through a cornfield and made it into the fort. But the men on foot had one killed and three wounded. They were forced to retreat, but kept up a rearguard of rifle fire to discourage pursuit. Allegedly, a rifle ball knocked Simon down. He was saved by a thick piece of sole leather he had in his shot pouch, where the bullet struck.

Caldwell then sent the majority of the warriors to raze nearby farms while the Rangers and the rest of the warriors kept the defenders in the fort pinned down. The marauders set fire to cabins and fields of crops, stole horses, and slaughtered more than three hundred hogs and 150 head of cattle. That night the warriors and Rangers ate well on pork and beef.

On the morning of August 17, Caldwell had to admit that without cannon, he couldn't take Bryan's Station in the time he had available. The fort had been reinforced, and no doubt there would be more Kentucky militia coming as word of the siege spread to other communities. Caldwell decided that it was time to withdraw. But as he had been successful in hiding the actual size of his force from the Americans, he put another plan into action.

Caldwell's army moved to a place by the Licking River known as Blue Licks, the site of a natural salt water spring or "lick." The army left an easy-to-follow trail, giving the impression that it was making a hasty retreat. Caldwell wanted the Americans to think that he had too few men to risk a battle.

Hours after Caldwell's withdrawal, a company of 170 volunteers led by Colonel John Todd arrived at Bryan's Station. With them were Daniel Boone and his twenty-one-year-old son, Israel. The rescuers stayed the night at the fort. The next day, believing the enemy was in flight from his superior numbers, Todd decided to go after them. Some of the men of Bryan's Station went along for what they were sure would be a trouncing of the Indians. But as they followed the trail, Daniel Boone had misgivings. The trail looked *too* clear for his liking.

The next morning, August 19, the Kentucky militia arrived at the Licking River. On a height on the other side of the river was Blue Licks. The column halted while the leaders decided whether or not to cross. A few warriors made an appearance on the opposite bank, then turned and fled into the forest — or so it appeared. Boone smelled a trap. He knew that somewhere behind them, Colonel Benjamin Logan was coming with another 150 men. Boone advised Todd to wait.

But an impulsive major named Hugh McGary didn't have the patience to listen to a veteran frontiersman like Boone. Colonel Todd had earlier accused McGary of timidity. Now McGary spurred his horse into the river, calling out, "Them that ain't cowards follow me!" Colonel Todd and his men surged after him. Against his better judgment, Daniel Boone went, too, with Israel beside him. Someone allegedly heard Boone say, "We are all slaughtered men," as he crossed the river.

The militiamen made the crossing without being fired upon. When they reached the other side, the majority of them dismounted and formed a battle line, as Todd suspected that the enemy was just up ahead. With Todd leading on horseback, they began to advance up the hill. Boone, who also had the rank of colonel, commanded the division on the left. He still had a gut feeling that they were walking into a trap. He was right!

When the Americans reached the summit, they were met with a withering volley of musket and rifle fire. Caldwell's Rangers and warriors blasted them from the cover of ravines and trees. Colonel Todd, an easy target astride his horse, was among the first to fall. Before the Americans could rally, a horde of shrieking warriors broke from concealment in the trees to the right of them.

In vicious hand-to-hand combat, the militia's right flank collapsed, quickly followed by the centre. Only the left flank, under

Boone, was holding its own. But with the rest of the militia force either dead or in terrified flight, his men were in danger of being cut off from the river and escape. Boone didn't realize that until panic-stricken Major McGary rode up and told him that the company was in full retreat, and he was surrounded.

Boone shouted to his men to withdraw. He caught a riderless horse and told Israel to get on and run for it, but Israel wouldn't abandon his father. While the elder Boone was trying to grab another horse, Israel was killed by a bullet through the neck. With no choice but to leave his son's body, Boone leapt onto the horse and fled with the remainder of the Kentucky militia.

The Battle of Blue Licks had lasted five minutes. When the gunsmoke cleared, seventy-seven Kentucky militiamen lay dead and six had been taken prisoner. Hugh McGary was among those who escaped. Caldwell's casualties were one Ranger and ten warriors killed, and fourteen warriors wounded.

Colonel Benjamin Logan had been hurrying to catch up with Todd's column when, six miles from the battle site, he ran into survivors fleeing from Blue Licks. Those men were unaware that Caldwell was the enemy commander, but some of them had seen Simon, conspicuous in his red bandana, in the thick of the fighting. They told Logan that Simon Girty and an overwhelming number of Indians had ambushed them.

Logan was stunned to hear of Todd's defeat, and he was alarmed at the news that the Indians were led by the White Savage. Fearing that Girty's warriors would come howling down the trail in pursuit of the routed militia, Logan ordered his men to take up defensive positions. Then he sent for reinforcements.

Five days later, Logan led 470 men to the Licking River. He sent two scouts across — Daniel Boone and Simon Kenton. The grieving Boone was looking for his son's body. Because of the effects of the summer heat and the ravages of animals, none of the human remains could be identified. They were buried in a mass grave. Kenton wondered when the day would come in which he and the man who was both his friend and enemy would meet on a battlefield.

The Americans contemplated another offensive against Sandusky, but once again could not raise enough volunteers. One militia officer wrote, "Simon Girty can outnumber him [General Irvine]; and, flushed with so many victories, to his natural boldness, he will be confident." The enormous sum of £1,500 was offered for anyone who brought Simon Girty in, dead or alive.

The clash at Blue Licks turned out to be the last significant battle of the American Revolutionary War. Ironically, it was a British-Native victory in a war the British had lost. Confirmation reached Detroit, and from there went to the towns of the Native allies, that following Cornwallis's surrender the British government was negotiating peace terms with the Americans. Major De Peyster had to recall an expedition guided by James Girty that had gone to attack Fort Henry at Wheeling. All American prisoners had to be turned over to the British for repatriation. Simon and the other agents were instructed to restrain the warriors, even though an army of over a thousand men led by George Rogers Clark had marched on Chillicothe. The people fled, and Clark's men burned the town and the fields of corn. The Americans had won the war in the east, but that did not mean that peace had come to the western frontier.

11

An Awkward Dilemma

The British commanders in Detroit and Niagara knew that Cornwallis's surrender was a grievous blow and that peace negotiations were under way. But they didn't know when, or even if, the war would be officially over. They found themselves in an awkward dilemma. Even as they told the Native leaders that the defeat at Yorktown was but a minor setback, they couldn't explain why the raiding had to stop. The chiefs were getting suspicious.

The Indian Department dismissed many of its agents. A few, like James and George Girty, were kept on at half pay. James and his wife set up a trading post in the Ohio country south of the Auglaize River. The Native community that grew around it became known as Girty's Town (now St. Mary's, Ohio). Simon was kept on at full pay with the rank of captain. Even though the fighting had stopped — for the moment — the British still had need of men like him, McKee, and Elliott.

Simon and his brothers couldn't return home. As far as the Americans were concerned, they were outlaws with bounties on their heads. They could expect nothing from their former countrymen but a firing squad or hanging. The British surrender had also left Simon with a difficult situation of another sort.

Simon didn't know that, without consulting the Native leaders, the British were signing away all claims to Native lands north of the Ohio River and as far west as the Mississippi. The Americans now considered those lands theirs by right of conquest. The British provided a large tract of land on the north shore of Lake Ontario and along the Grand River, in what soon would be called Upper Canada, for Joseph Brant and his people, who had lost their home in New York's Mohawk Valley.

No such provision was made for the tribes of the western frontier. They had fought the Americans to a standstill and were still in possession of their ancestral homelands. Simon certainly would have wondered what an American victory would mean to *them*. Would the British still be their ally against American expansion? Or would his adopted people be betrayed?

Simon didn't know that the Natives hadn't been considered *at all* in the negotiations between the British and Americans. He knew only that he had orders to convince the chiefs to restrain their warriors from raiding and to send all of their white captives to Detroit. When the chiefs asked Simon how matters stood in their alliance with the king, he could give them only vague answers. There was one thing Simon did know for certain: the Americans coveted Native lands, and the tribes would not give them up without a fight, with or without British help.

In April 1783, General Sir Frederick Haldimand, the Governor General of British North America, wanted to know what the Americans were up to. Even though a truce was in effect, as far as he knew, they were still at war. He wrote to De Peyster, suggesting that he send "an intelligent" agent to spy on Pittsburgh and if possible bring back a prisoner. Simon got the assignment and set off with seventeen Wyandot warriors.

The spy party arrived in the vicinity of Pittsburgh undetected. On May 5, near Simon's old home at Squirrel Hill, they captured fourteen-year-old John Burkhart. As they started back for Detroit, they heard the big guns of the fort being fired. Simon asked John what that was for. The boy replied that the people of Pittsburgh were celebrating the end of the war.

Someone had seen the Wyandots seize John, and the local people immediately assumed that Simon Girty was with them. A group of forty to fifty men gathered to decide what should be done. They came to the conclusion that Girty's half-brother, John Turner Jr., must also have been involved. He still lived at the Squirrel Hill homestead with his elderly mother. Someone suggested that they march on Squirrel Hill, put Turner's farm to the torch, and either drive him out of the country or hang him as a traitor. A friend of Turner's spoke strongly against this.

While the argument was still ongoing, someone told Turner about the meeting. He went right out to face his accusers. He angrily told them that if they didn't trust him and wouldn't leave him alone, he would go over to the British, not by choice, but because they had forced him. Impressed by this show of courage, the men took back their accusations and allowed him to return home without further trouble.

It isn't known if Simon had taken the opportunity to secretly visit his mother and half-brother, but considering Simon's bold nature and the fact that the war had not severed the strong ties of the Girty-Turner family, it's quite likely that he did.

News that the peace treaty had been signed reached Detroit on May 6. De Peyster arranged for meetings with the principal chiefs. Governor Haldimand had instructed him not to tell them any of the details of the treaty. At the council that was held in mid-June, De Peyster sat as the representative of the king, with Simon translating. Chief Half King spoke for the Wyandots.

> Father!
> Listen to me since this is the day that the Great Spirit has allowed us to meet you in this Council House where you have seen us often assembled.

> Father!
> These strings [of wampum] were delivered us by Simon Girty whom you sent to acquaint us that it was your desire we should sit still and not go to war until we had heard from You. There are the strings and we have listened to them. You also desired that we should send a few young men by Simon Girty in order to get a prisoner to give you intelligence. You were so particular as to Desire that none might go on this errand that had lost friends in the war. That, Father, would have been a difficult matter as most of our nation have suffered.

Half King and the rest of the chiefs wanted to know the truth of what was happening between the British and the Americans, but De Peyster was under orders to disclose nothing and to make no promises. Even more troubling for De Peyster was the fact that hundreds of American captives were still in remote Native villages. Simon and the handful of agents still on the Indian Department payroll had the huge task of travelling through the wilderness to find them, convince their captors to release them, and then put them on the long trails that would take them to Detroit and eventually their homes.

By July Simon was back in Detroit. He was ill, but he was needed as the principal translator at yet another important council. Chiefs representing eleven tribes were there to listen to the British Superintendent General of Indian Affairs, Sir John Johnson, son of the late Sir William Johnson. Also present was an American envoy, Major Ephraim Douglas.

Johnson told the assembled chiefs that the British had made peace with the Americans, and that they should do so, too. The king would no longer be able to assist them if they made war. Nonetheless, the tribes should be ready to defend their lands if the Americans invaded.

De Peyster and Johnson wouldn't allow Major Douglas to address the chiefs. They were afraid that he would tell them the truth about the peace treaty: that the British had ceded Native lands to the Americans as though they were the king's to give away — which they weren't! De Peyster made sure that the chiefs had no access to the major. When Douglas protested, De Peyster said the American would have to speak to his superior, General Allan MacLean at Niagara.

Douglas and his escort left for Niagara on July 7. Simon was too ill to make the trip. He might have been suffering from his head injury, or he might have been taken down by a local epidemic. In Niagara, Douglas found General MacLean just as unwilling to let him address the chiefs as De Peyster had been. In frustration, Douglas took passage on a ship across Lake Ontario to Oswego, but somehow the Natives learned the shocking truth about the peace treaty.

Still in his sickbed, Simon heard of the rumours that were sweeping the country from Quebec City to Detroit — that the British had abandoned the Natives and that the new United States of America had declared that every tribe that had fought for the British had to move to Canada or across the Mississippi. Like the chiefs, Simon was outraged at this betrayal. But he also knew that the Natives were in no position to break off their friendly relations with the British. He began to sense, as did many of the tribal leaders, that in order to defend themselves against the Americans, the tribes would have to follow the example of the American colonies and unite.

In an attempt to ease Native anger, Sir John Johnson told a council of chiefs at Niagara that the peace treaty had nothing to do with their rights to their own lands. It was just a matter of setting boundaries, he said. Indian land was still Indian land! He pleaded with the chiefs to not attack the Americans, but at the same time to be ready to fight invaders.

Joseph Brant led a delegation of chiefs who wanted to organize a Native confederation even larger than that of the Iroquois Confederacy. The British liked the idea. They saw a strong "United States of Indians" as a first line of defence against an American invasion of Canada. As a show of support, the British sent a shipload of gifts to Niagara, to be distributed among the Natives who would be gathering at Lower Sandusky for the council meetings.

By mid-August Simon had recovered from his illness. He was in Detroit when he learned that Joseph Brant would be visiting en route to Sandusky with about fifty other Iroquois delegates. Simon hadn't seen Brant in the two years since the Mohawk chief had almost killed him. He'd been told that Brant had expressed deep regret over what he had done. Nonetheless, Simon had been waiting a long time for the opportunity to confront Brant. He thought about it every time he looked in a mirror at the ugly scar Brant's sword had left on his head, and every time he was laid low by murderous headaches.

Photo courtesy of the Brant Historical Society.

Joseph Brant, the great Mohawk war chief, was a driving force behind the plan to form a Native confederation, but in a drunken dispute he almost killed Simon with a sword stroke to the head.

Brant and his party arrived at Detroit on August 18. The chief was in his lodging, preparing for some business he had with De Peyster, when the door swung open. Standing in the doorway was Simon Girty, his head covered with the red bandana that hid his scar.

Both men held the rank of captain. If they had been any other British officers with a dispute to settle, one would have struck the other on the cheek with a glove and challenged him to a duel. They would have appointed friends to act as seconds. Then they would have arranged to meet somewhere outside the fort on the "field of honour" to settle the matter with swords or pistols. But this was the frontier, and a man like Simon had no use for gentlemanly etiquette when it came to a fight.

Simon strode into the room and laid two pistols and two swords on a table.

"I'll have satisfaction of you, Brant," he said. "Choose the weapons, and we'll fight it out, here and now. But you'll have to face me like a man, instead of sneaking up from behind like a coward."

Brant didn't reach for a weapon. Instead, he begged Simon's forgiveness. Simon gave it, and a confrontation that might have turned bloody ended quietly. But from that time on, Simon had no respect for Brant — he considered him a coward. It was also said that Brant would never allow himself to be alone with Simon Girty.

In spite of the personal animosity between Simon and Brant, each was aware of the importance of the other in the hope of creating a grand Native confederation. Brant knew that Simon was the best agent and interpreter the British Indian Department had. No other white man on the western frontier was held in higher regard in Native communities. Simon, for his part, knew that there could be no confederacy without Brant and the Six Nations. The British and all the other chiefs recognized Brant as a strong leader. Like Simon, he was a gifted orator whose words could move those who might be indecisive. For the common good, the two men would have to put their differences aside and work together. The future of the Western tribes, and perhaps even Canada, depended on it.

While preparations were being made for the big council at Sandusky, Simon was surprised by the sudden arrival at Detroit in mid-August of his brother Thomas and half-brother John Turner. They told him that they were interested in acquiring land in Canada. They said that their neighbours had treated them poorly because of their relationship to the outlaw Girty brothers. Thomas and John had come to Detroit as representatives of other Pennsylvanians who were being persecuted as suspected Tories. They wanted to see what "encouragement" there might be for them to move to Canada and live under the British flag.

Simon was overjoyed to see his brothers. He sent word to James and George, who hurried to Detroit for a family reunion. For a few days the three most notorious men on the frontier and their two "Patriot" siblings enjoyed each other's company. They drank in the taverns and talked about old times. Simon, James, and George tried to impress upon Thomas and John the benefits of moving to Canada.

At the end of August, with Thomas and John still undecided, Simon had to leave for the council at Sandusky. Drawn by the promise of British gifts and interest in a proposed confederation to stand against the land-hungry Americans, delegates had come from all of the Ohio country tribes and from the Great Lakes region. There were even Creeks and Cherokees from as far away as Florida. The Senecas were represented, but Simon saw with regret that his old mentor Guyasuta was not present. He'd been hoping that they might be reconciled.

Speaking for the Crown were Alexander McKee, newly appointed as Deputy Agent for Indian Affairs; Matthew Elliott, now head of all Indian agents; and Lieutenant W. Johnson of the Royal British Marines. Although he shared the task of translating the many speeches with others, Simon was the principal interpreter. He repeated in various languages McKee's message that the king still considered the tribes as his faithful allies. McKee urged them to lay down the tomahawk, release all white prisoners, and make peace with the Americans, but to defend themselves if invaded. The king, he said, still wanted their trade, and would provide "all other benefits in his power." That was a strong suggestion that if it came to war with the Americans, the British would still supply the warriors with guns, ammunition, and other necessities.

Then Brant called upon the assembled chiefs to commit themselves and their peoples to the confederation that he said was their only hope of survival.

> Brothers and nephews. You the Hurons, Delawares, Shawnese, Mingoes, Ottawas, Chippeweys [*sic*], Pouttewatamies [*sic*], Creeks and Cherokees. We the Six Nations with this belt bind your Hearts and minds with ours, that there may be never hereafter a separation between us, let there be Peace or War, it shall never disunite us, for our Interests are alike, nor should anything ever be done but by the voice of the whole as we make but one with you.

The chiefs were receptive to Brant's appeal. Some of them were already having trouble with Americans who considered themselves homesteaders and settlers, but whom the Natives saw as squatters. Speaking to McKee and Brant, Chief Half King said what was on the minds of most of his colleagues.

> Father! Listen! As also our Brethren the Six Nations, you have told us there is peace. You know the Rights of our Indians in this Country, and you know that the Tomahawk is now laid down. Brethren the Six Nations, you know where the Boundary Line was fixed, since you were the people who fixed it. We now inform you that the Virginians are already encroaching upon our Lands, we desire you and our Father to be strong, and desire them to desist from encroaching upon us, otherwise, they will destroy the good work of Peace which we are endeavoring to promote. This is all that we have to say.

McKee and Elliott distributed the British gifts, and Brant closed the conference by symbolically binding the nations. He promised that the Six Nations would confront the Americans over the encroaching Virginians. The council had been a tremendous success, with thirty-five nations pledged to stand united. Officially, Simon had only been an interpreter. But in such a high-level conference in which every word was important, the interpreter's job was vital. Moreover, the chiefs knew that Simon favoured the confederation, and his opinion carried a lot of weight with them. He had worked well with Brant, and thus by example demonstrated that personal quarrels should not undermine cooperation.

As the delegates all set off on their journeys home, they knew that the spirit of cooperation would soon be tested. No one doubted that the Americans would do everything they could to destroy the confederation.

12

Simon and Catherine

When Simon returned to Detroit, he was disappointed to learn that John Turner had decided not to move to Canada after all. There was a young woman back in Pittsburgh he had made up his mind to marry, so he was going home. Simon wished his half-brother well, and arranged for an escort to take him safely through Native territory.

A few weeks later, Thomas also decided that he preferred to live under the American flag. Simon accompanied Thomas and some companions as far as Sandusky, where two Delawares agreed to join them on the trail. Then Simon wished Thomas a safe journey. Both partings were hard ones, because the brothers didn't know when, or if, they would see each other again.

The peace in the Ohio country was at best an uneasy one. In spite of pledges made to Brant and McKee at Sandusky, some tribes made territorial concessions to the Americans. In the wake of the British defeat, the chiefs feared American military might. In the autumn of 1783, they didn't realize that neither the new American government nor the individual states were in a position to fight the united tribes. They were short of both money and soldiers. President George Washington, on the advice of his generals, endorsed a strategy that he hoped would "preserve American peace while taking Indian land."

The idea was that the United States could advance its borders without fighting the Natives or even paying them anything for their land. All the American negotiators had to do was promise to allow the Natives to continue living on land they ceded to the Americans. Settlers would then move in. The presence of settlers, who cut down the forests to make farmland, always drove away the game upon which the Natives depended. With no game to hunt, the Natives would have no choice but to move away.

But the Americans soon learned that it wasn't going to be that easy. After a while, the chiefs began to realize that the Americans didn't have a big army posed for invasion. If they did, why hadn't they used it to drive the British out of the Ohio country? According to the peace treaty, the British were supposed to abandon all of their western posts, including Detroit. But Detroit was still in British hands. The traders moving among the villages and setting up posts were British and Canadians, working for men like McKee and Elliott. American negotiators found the chiefs becoming stubbornly defiant in the face of intimidation.

Even though the situation on the frontier was smouldering, and the British were refusing to live up to their agreement to get out of the western forts, the officers in Detroit and Niagara were nonetheless anxious to fulfill the part of the treaty that called for the release of all American captives. In spite of the best efforts of Simon and other agents, many people remained unaccounted for. Americans frequently went to Detroit, clinging to hopes that lost family members might still be alive somewhere in the wilderness. Even though throughout the American settlements the name "Girty" inspired terror and disgust, some of the Americans arriving in Detroit who had known Simon before the war did not believe that he was the monster the tall tales told of. They also knew that if anyone could find their missing kinfolk, it was he.

Finding and identifying captives could be difficult, especially if they had been taken as small children and held for years. There were no pictures to go by, and verbal descriptions could be of little help if the person had matured. Sometimes children who had been adopted and raised by Native parents could no longer understand English and had even forgotten the names with which they'd been christened.

In November, Simon was asked to find an eighteen-year-old girl named Catherine Malott. Her mother, Sarah, had gone to Detroit seeking help. Catherine had been captured three-and-a-half years earlier in an attack on a little flotilla of boats on the Ohio River. The raiders had been a mixed band of Delawares, Wyandots, and Mingoes. For Simon, knowing exactly when and where the attack had occurred and which tribes' warriors had been involved was an important starting point. But the trail could still be a long one, because the warriors often sold or gave captives away.

It wasn't recorded just when or where Simon found Catherine. What is known is that he "fell hard" for her the moment he set eyes on her. According to everyone who knew her, Catherine Malott was extraordinarily beautiful. She was tall with dark hair and brown eyes. She was nineteen by the time Simon, forty-three, located her in a Shawnee village.

Simon either bought Catherine's freedom or tricked the Shawnees into letting him take her. He allegedly told her captors that he wanted to take the girl to Detroit to visit her aging mother, and that he would then return her. Simon and Catherine set out with some other freed captives on the long trail to Detroit. By the time Simon delivered Catherine into the arms of her weeping mother in Detroit in the spring of 1784, the young woman was as much in love with the dark-eyed frontiersman who had rescued her as he was with her.

In August, with Sarah Malott's blessing, Simon and Catherine were married. In spite of the difference in their ages, the newly-weds had some key things in common. Each had lived in both the white and Native worlds. Simon had known what it was to be an outcast. Catherine was no doubt aware that because of the years she had spent living among the Natives, there would be those in white society who would look upon her with condescension.

Now that he had a wife to care for, Simon had to think about settling down. As an agent of the British Indian Department who had served faithfully and with distinction during the war, he was entitled to apply for a grant of land on the Canadian side of the Detroit River. He received a 164-acre lot overlooking Lake Erie, right at the river mouth. Among the Girtys' neighbours were Alexander McKee, Matthew Elliott, Henry Bird, and William Caldwell. Their homesteads were the beginning of the Township of Malden.

Simon built a two-storey frame house and began having land cleared for farming. The Girty home in Canada, just like the old Girty home in Pennsylvania, welcomed many visitors, both white and Native. Catherine was always a gracious hostess. In the spring of 1785, their first child, John, was born, but the happiness in the Girty household was short-lived. Just a few months later, the baby became ill and died. At about the same time, although the grieving Simon wouldn't get the news for several months, Mary Girty-Turner died at Squirrel Hill.

Soon after the loss of their first-born, Simon had to leave Catherine to mourn and manage the farm alone. He had been summoned back to work. Sir John Johnson and McKee wanted him to travel throughout the Ohio country, encouraging the various tribes to stand firm with the confederation. American commissioners had been visiting the villages, trying to argue the chiefs into giving up more land. On a few occasions, Simon met some of the Americans in Native communities. Some were men he had known before the war, and they got along cordially, despite being there at cross-purposes. Simon even assisted them in recovering captives. Of course, other Americans Simon encountered would have dearly wished they could seize him and haul him back to Pittsburgh. But among Simon's Native friends, they didn't dare. They could only carry back reports of his activities to American authorities. Lieutenant Colonel Josiah Harmar, commander of the First American Regiment at Fort Pitt, singled Simon out in a report to the Secretary of War.

> Speeches have been continually sent by the British from Detroit to the Indians since the treaty, and I have good intelligence that several traders have been among them, using all means to make them entertain a bad opinion of the Americans. One Simon Girty, I am informed, has been to Sandusky for that purpose. I have taken every means in my power to counteract their proceedings, and have directed the Indians not to listen to their lies, but to tie and bring in

here any of those villains who spread reports
among them injurious to the United States, in
order that they may be punished.

Harmar was relatively new to the western frontier, and evidently not aware that the warriors were hardly likely to tie up "one Simon Girty" and bring him in. On the contrary, they were paying close attention to what Simon had to say. The Wyandots and Delawares began to raid Americans who were illegally squatting on the Native side of the Ohio River. The Mingoes captured a young man named John Crawford (no relation to Colonel William Crawford) who was trespassing on their territory. At a meeting with American commissioners, at which Simon interpreted, a Mingo chief named Captain Johnny released Crawford to them as a sign of good faith, but with a warning.

Keep your people within bounds or we will take
up a Rod and whip them back to your side of
the Ohio ... Listen to us, otherwise the consequences of what may happen hereafter will be
your fault ... we have called in Simon Girty
that our words should be fully explained to you
before him.

Meanwhile, the Shawnees had resumed raiding the Americans. To their surprise, no American army came to take revenge. Perhaps the Long Knives weren't as powerful as everyone had feared! But in some places the American strategy of ecological warfare — the destruction of the forests and the driving away of game — was starting to take effect.

A band of about three hundred Shawnee men, women, and children led by an old chief named Moluntha responded to an invitation to meet American commissioners at Fort Finney, near present day Cincinnati, Ohio. Most of the other Shawnee chiefs had ignored the summons, but Moluntha and a few others were in desperate need of food and other supplies. On January 18, 1786, Moluntha and a handful of chiefs sat down in council with commissioners Richard Butler, Samuel Holden Parsons, and George Rogers Clark.

Even though these chiefs were not there as representatives of the Shawnee nation, Butler demanded that they sign a treaty that gave huge tracts of land to the United States. The chiefs protested. "God gave us this country!" Chief Kekewpellethy declared. "We do not understand measuring out the land. It is all ours."

Butler said that the land belonged to the United States and that the Shawnees, "instead of persisting in your folly, should be thankful for the forgiveness and offers of kindness of the United States."

Chief Kekewpellethy once again denounced the treaty. Then he presented Butler with a string of black wampum, which was a symbolic threat of war. Butler's response was that if the Shawnees wanted war, it could begin at once. He contemptuously dashed the wampum string against the council table and then stalked out. Clark swept the string off the table with his cane, and crushed it underfoot as he, too, stormed out of the room.

This display of anger and contempt stunned the chiefs. The next time they met with Butler they were contrite. Butler produced the document, and the chiefs put their marks on it. By the end of January, the commissioners had cowed several other chiefs into signing. But these chiefs did not by any means represent the confederation. Since the end of the Revolutionary War, the Ohio country had been a powder keg. The so-called Treaty of Fort Finney was the fuse that ignited it.

With the Americans declaring the newly acquired territory formally theirs by right of treaty, settlers began moving in. Angry Native leaders of all tribes denounced the treaty as a fraud and vowed to fight it. With the coming of spring, Simon, McKee and Elliott were once again travelling amongst the tribes, urging them to resist the Americans. Catherine, pregnant again, faced more months of loneliness. In Pittsburgh, George Rogers Clark was arguing for a military strike against the western tribes to show them that the United States was prepared to go to war.

Simon, McKee, and Elliott were in Sandusky in June when they received a message from Sir John Johnson to report to Niagara. Councils were being held there with the Six Nations, Shawnees, Ottawas, Chippewas, and Wyandots. Simon had been away from home for months, and was looking forward to spending at least a little time with Catherine, but he was obliged to go to Niagara, where he was needed as interpreter. On June 19, 1786, while Simon was doing his duty in Niagara, hundreds of miles away his name was being spoken in the American Congress.

> The deponent saith … That Simon Girty, another of the said emissaries, had said in public where he, the deponent was, that he was sent from Detroit to prevent the Indians from attending the treaty with the United States, which was to be held at the Miami.

Officials at the highest levels of power were becoming aware of just how much of a thorn in the side of the United States Simon Girty was. Many of them were men who, during the

Revolutionary War, had paid little attention to the struggle on the western frontier. They began to see Simon as equal in villainy to that other notorious turncoat, Benedict Arnold!

The tribes escalated their raids. On June 30, Congress ordered Colonel Harmar to Louisville, Kentucky, with two companies of federal infantry. This small force was to be supplemented by Kentucky militia. George Rogers Clark was made commander-in-chief. Among the militia officers were Colonel Benjamin Logan, Colonel Daniel Boone, and Major Simon Kenton.

Clark planned a two-pronged attack. Setting out in early October, he and Logan led separate columns into enemy territory. Because of a dry summer the rivers were low. Supply boats couldn't reach their destinations, and Clark's advance ground to a halt. Without food, many of the militiamen either deserted or threatened mutiny. Clark was forced to withdraw before his men had so much as fired a shot. Simon, who had been sent to spy on Clark, watched the Americans retreat, and then headed back to Sandusky to report. There he learned from Native runners that Logan's column had been more successful.

With Simon Kenton and Daniel Boone working as scouts, Logan had caught the Shawnee towns on the Mad River by surprise. He struck just when a major council was about to take place. Joseph Brant was present, along with the leaders of several western tribes. By the time the smoke cleared, twenty warriors were dead and eighty had been taken prisoner. Brant himself narrowly escaped capture. Logan burned eight Shawnee towns and all of the adjacent cornfields. Then he and his men quickly withdrew.

Logan's victory didn't diminish the Shawnee will to fight. On the contrary, it made them and the other confederation tribes all the more determined to resist. In Sandusky, Simon dictated a letter to McKee, informing him off all that had happened regarding Clark and Logan. Meanwhile, back in the Girty farmhouse in Canada, Catherine gave birth to their second child, Nancy Anne.

13

Return of the White Savage

When Simon finally returned home in November, he was thrilled to find that he was the father of a lovely little daughter, but he also soon learned just how hard his long absences had been on Catherine. Simon had hired men to do the actual work on the farm, so Catherine's daily chores had been no more than those of any other pioneer housewife. Nonetheless, she had been lonely, and she blamed Simon. Now she was distant with him. It didn't help matters when scarcely a week after Simon's return McKee called him back to Detroit.

Yet another big council was being held, with chiefs representing the Six Nations, Wabash, Cherokees, Wyandots, Shawnees, Delawares, Ottawas, Miamis, Chippewas, Delawares, and Potawatomies. They were there to decide whether they should continue to fight the Americans or make peace with them. Brant, as both a chief and an officer of the Crown, officiated at the meetings. Officially, Simon was an interpreter. But along with McKee and Elliott, he was there to encourage the chiefs to uphold their pledges to the confederation and keep fighting.

There was disagreement from the start. Most of the Delawares and Wyandots wanted to make peace with the Americans. The rest were for war. After a month of speeches, debate, and argument, the delegates reached a compromise. They agreed on a carefully worded message to the American Congress. It said that the Native Confederation considered recent treaties the Americans had imposed upon chiefs to be invalid. The Americans were to honour their old agreement that the Ohio River was a permanent boundary. They requested that the United States send officials to meet the chiefs at a halfway location acceptable to both sides. In the meantime, no more surveyors or settlers were to cross the Ohio River, unless the Americans wanted war.

The letter was sent to Congress, where it was ignored. The British agents and the chiefs waited for months for a reply that would never come. In January 1787, the governor of Virginia announced that the lands north of the Ohio River were open for settlement.

In the early months of 1787, Simon spent as much time at home as he could trying to mend his relationship with Catherine, but McKee was constantly summoning him across the river to Detroit. On one occasion, while his own family life was in need of attention, Simon was called upon to help another family. James and Mary Moore were teenagers who had been taken captive by Natives. James had been sold to a French Canadian who lived near Detroit, and Mary to a Loyalist named Stockwell whose farm was not far away. James was well-treated by his owner, but he learned that Mary was suffering from abuse and neglect at the hands of her master. James appealed to Simon for help. Thanks to the intervention of Simon and McKee, James and Mary Moore were both released from servitude and went back to their home in Virginia.

In spite of the warning in the confederation's letter to Congress, boatloads of settlers crossed the Ohio. On July 13, 1787, Congress formally annexed the territory it claimed was American by right of treaty. President Washington appointed General Arthur St. Clair as its first governor. He was a Scottish-born veteran of the Seven Years' War and the Revolutionary War who, in spite of having once been brought before a courts martial, Washington held in high esteem. St. Clair was ambitious, aggressive, and had no regard for Natives.

In the early autumn of 1787, delegates from most of the confederated tribes were gathered at the Foot of the Rapids of the Maumee River, still expecting to meet American representatives. With them were Brant, McKee, and Simon. When no Wyandot or Delaware chiefs showed up, McKee feared that their absence would show a rift in the confederation that the Americans would try to exploit. He sent Simon to Sandusky to convince the chiefs of the importance of their presence. Once again, Simon's diplomatic skills were successful. Wyandot and Delaware representatives accompanied him back to the Maumee.

Weeks passed with no word from the Americans, even after Brant and McKee sent another letter to Congress. This was an enormous insult to all of the chiefs. Frustrated and angry, they returned to their homes after agreeing to meet again at the same place a year later.

Simon hurried back to Malden. This time he and Catherine resolved their problems. Home was once again comfortable for the middle-aged frontiersman and his young wife. By mid-November,

Catherine was again with child. Nine months later she gave birth to a boy, named Thomas after his uncle.

In the months following the arrival of little Thomas Girty, the situation on the frontier remained volatile. Governor St. Clair and Commissioner Richard Butler were pushy and overbearing in their dealings with the tribes. Congress feared an "Indian war" which the United States at the time had neither the money nor the military power to pursue. In a complete reversal of attitude, Congress and Secretary of War Henry Knox pressured St. Clair and Butler into inviting chiefs from the Mohawks, Senecas, Wyandots, Delawares, Miamis, and Shawnees to peace talks at the Falls of the Muskingum River.

Advised by Brant, the representatives of the invited tribes agreed to meet at the Foot of the Rapids on the Maumee to discuss policies before confronting the Americans. Simon, James, and George all attended that meeting. They sided with McKee in encouraging the chiefs to stand up to the Americans, even though Brant now talked about making concessions. When the meeting was over, Simon rushed home for his son's first birthday.

While the chiefs were deliberating by the Maumee, a small company of American soldiers was sent to the Falls of the Muskingum to build a council house and a warehouse for the presents the commissioners would distribute among the Natives. While the soldiers worked, a war party of about a dozen Chippewas suddenly attacked. Two soldiers and one black slave were killed, and three others were wounded before the warriors were driven off with gunfire.

When Governor St. Clair was told of the attack he was furious. He sent an angry message to the chiefs, accusing them of murder and treachery. He emphasized that the council fire at the Falls of the Muskingum was now permanently extinguished. The chiefs replied that the Chippewa warriors were renegades who had acted completely on their own and not with the approval of the confederation. They still wanted to meet the Americans at the Falls of the Muskingum. St. Clair insisted on a location more favourable to the Americans, but the chiefs wouldn't agree to that. Several of them went home.

St. Clair learned through his agents — spies who were passing themselves off as traders — that the Senecas, Wyandots, and Delawares were wavering in their support of war, and that Brant was working desperately to hold the confederation together. The governor mistakenly believed that the confederacy was all but finished. He sent agents to the Senecas, Wyandots, and Delawares, inviting them to a council at Fort Harmar, a new post at the mouth of the Muskingum River.

Only two hundred men, women and children responded to the invitation, arriving at Fort Harmar in mid-December. But St. Clair was less interested in numbers than he was in getting signatures on treaty documents; signatures that the American government could point to as "proof" of its "legal" ownership of disputed lands. On January 9, 1789, several chiefs who had decided that further resistance to the Americans was futile, placed their marks on the Fort Harmar treaties. Among them were Simon's old friends Captain Pipe and Half King, and his estranged adopted father, Guyasuta. These chiefs hoped that they and their people could now live in an honourable peace with the United States. They were as much mistaken as St. Clair, who believed — and bragged — that he had convinced the western tribes, once and for all, that the Ohio country was now American soil.

At the time that the Fort Harmar treaties were being signed, Simon was at his home in Malden. He'd grown tired of waiting for American diplomats who didn't show, and weary of the bickering within the confederation. He was forty-eight years old, and he wanted to spend time with his family. Simon stayed in Malden for all of 1789, not venturing any farther than Detroit, where he was still on the payroll as an interpreter. But that didn't prevent him from being blamed for atrocities committed hundreds of miles away.

Native anger over treaties that were nothing but land grabs resulted in an escalation of bloody raids against settlers on the north side of the Ohio River. Members of farm families were killed and scalped, or taken captive. In one alleged attack on a homestead, a warrior killed a young girl with his tomahawk. The story spread that the villainous Simon Girty was the leader of the war party.

In April 1790, General Josiah Harmar decided to lead a punitive expedition of 120 regular troops and about two hundred Kentucky militiamen against warriors camped at the mouth of the Scioto River. They had been attacking settlers coming down the Ohio River. At the approach of Harmar's column, the warriors simply vanished into the forest. After tramping through the woods for two weeks and finding no Indians to kill, the militiamen grumbled that they wanted to go home. Harmar reluctantly called a halt to his expedition and turned back. A few weeks later, the warriors he had been hunting were back at the mouth of the Scioto. They attacked a flotilla of six federal boats, killing five men and taking eight more prisoner.

In May, Simon was interpreting for delegates from several confederated tribes who had gone to Detroit to see how their relationship with the British stood. Before long, McKee was again sending him on missions into the Ohio country. On one of those excursions, Simon was directly responsible for rescuing the children of John and Elizabeth Quick from captivity. Ten children had been taken early in the year, and Simon managed to buy back some of them. When the captors of the others wouldn't sell the children, Simon stole them back. He was able to return nine to their parents. One girl was never recovered.

In the autumn of 1790, Governor St. Clair and General Harmar prepared for a two-pronged attack on the Native communities at the St. Joseph and St. Mary's rivers. There were Shawnee and Delaware villages, but the largest was the Miami town of Kekionga. Secretary of War Henry Knox didn't want to alarm the British, so he sent a message to Detroit advising Major Patrick Murray that the military expedition was aimed strictly at hostile Natives, and not at any British posts. He requested that the British not assist or alert the Natives. Major Murray promptly informed McKee, who in turn sent Simon to warn the Natives.

On September 30, Major John Hamtramck's column of five hundred men, four hundred of whom were militia, set out from Vincennes. This was a diversionary thrust. By the time the column reached a Kickapoo village on the Vermillion River ten days later, many of the militiamen had deserted. The village had been abandoned, but the remainder of the militiamen feared that hundreds of warriors were waiting in ambush just ahead. They would go no further. Hamtramck had no choice but to withdraw.

Five days later, General Harmar's army of 1,500, of whom only three hundred were regular troops, arrived at the Miami villages 150 miles away. Here, too, the inhabitants had fled, after first setting the buildings on fire. There was nothing for Harmar's frustrated men to do but burn the cornfields.

On October 19, in hope that the expedition wouldn't be a complete failure, Harmer sent Colonel John Hardin with thirty regulars and 150 militiamen to see if he could make contact with the enemy. Seven miles from Kekionga, the Miami war chief Little Turtle cleverly drew Hardin's company into an ambush. In a clash that is now known as the Battle of Heller's Corner, all but eight of the American regulars were killed. Of the militiamen, most of whom ran for their lives at the first crack of gunfire, forty were killed and a dozen wounded.

On the morning of October 22, Little Turtle's warriors and some Shawnee allies handed Harmar's army a stunning defeat, with over 180 men killed or wounded. Native losses were relatively light. The Miamis and Shawnees called it the Battle of the Pumpkin Fields, because the steam rising from the scalped skulls of the fallen Americans reminded them of mist in a pumpkin field on a frosty autumn morning.

These setbacks were humiliating to the Americans and greatly encouraging to the Natives. Now the concept of a strong confederation looked better than ever. To support the Natives' high level of confidence, the British in Detroit sent food, clothing, and ammunition to the people of Kekionga, who they knew would be suffering after having their cornfields burned.

In mid-November Simon was present when the chiefs of the confederated tribes gathered on the banks of the Maumee to discuss their next steps. He suggested that speeches be sent far and wide, calling on warriors to assemble there in the spring to repel the American invasion that was almost certainly coming. The chiefs agreed. They also chose a delegation to go to Quebec City and seek the assistance of the governor, Lord Dorchester. When Simon proposed a winter strike against the Americans, the chiefs not only agreed, but also asked Simon to lead the war party. It was a significant honour that indicated the high level of respect they had for him.

Two targets were selected for simultaneous attacks: Baker's Station on the Virginia side of the Ohio River, and Dunlap's Station on the east side of the Great Miami River. These forts were many miles apart, and the matter concerning which war party Simon was actually with would become a matter of controversy in the legend of the White Savage.

Early in the morning of January 8, 1791, warriors attacked a four-man surveying party not far from Dunlap's Station. One man was killed. Two others managed to escape. They made it to the fort and raised the alarm. The fourth man, Abner Hunt, was captured.

Huddled inside the wooden walls of Dunlap's Station were women, children, and about thirty-five men and older boys. The commander was Lieutenant Jacob Kingsbury of the U.S. Army. When three days passed with no attack, Kingsbury assumed that the surveyors had been the victims of a small raiding party. But on the morning of the fourth day, warriors surrounded the post.

They brought Abner Hunt out to where the defenders could see him. Hunt called out that the warriors demanded the fort's surrender. Kingsbury refused, saying that he had already sent a messenger for help. The warriors then opened fire, and in the gun battle that followed several of them were killed or

Little Turtle, the Miami chief who defeated General Harmar and General St. Clair.

wounded. In the fort there were two casualties, one of them fatal.

The siege of Dunlap's Station lasted a little over twenty-four hours. When the Natives failed to set the fort ablaze with fire arrows, they turned to slaughtering all of the cattle in the vicinity. At one point a warrior who seemed to be the leader called to Kingsbury by name, and said that Simon Girty was with them.

Then, before giving up on the attack, the warriors killed Abner Hunt. Kingsbury wrote in his report, "Hunt, the prisoner, they murdered within two hundred yards of the garrison." In many accounts Hunt was tortured horribly, and the people in the garrison could hear his screams throughout the night. But in a report that is detailed in many other respects, Kingsbury makes no mention of torture. He says only that Hunt was "murdered." Moreover, in the various stories that have Hunt being tortured to death, the narrators differ on the form of the torture; all of which cast doubt on their reliability.

At no point in his report does Kingsbury say that he actually saw or heard Simon Girty. He says only that the Native leader *said* that Girty was with them. In other attacks on forts, Simon had stood forth and identified himself. That he did not do so at Dunlap's Station was quite likely because he wasn't there! The Native leader, who was probably the Shawnee Chief Blue Jacket, was evidently trying to use a little psychological warfare, knowing the fear in which the Americans held Simon.

At about the same time that Dunlap's Station came under siege, the other war party attacked Baker's Station. The garrison had been warned, so any chance of surprise was lost. As warriors surrounded the post, a white man called out for its surrender. Men in the fort recognized the voice of Simon Girty, and answered him with curses. The fort was under fire for a day and a night, with no casualties, before the attackers withdrew.

Simon couldn't have been at both Dunlap's Station and Baker's Station at the same time, and the evidence indicates that he was at Baker's. Nonetheless, the story spread that he was at Dunlap's, and that he was responsible for Abner Hunt's terrible death by torture. As with the death of Colonel Crawford, no one questioned the veracity of the story. As far as the American settlers were concerned, the White Savage had returned!

14

The Battle of the Wabash

The Natives didn't hold Simon responsible for the failures at Dunlap's and Baker's Stations. In both cases the defenders had been alerted, and the warriors didn't have the supplies to sustain them over a long siege. Simon was glad to be back in Malden in time for the birth of his and Catherine's second daughter, Sarah, on April 18, 1791.

That spring Simon gained some new neighbours. The Moravian missionary Reverend David Zeisberger had been living with his flock of Native converts in a community called New Salem on the Pequotting River. With the threat of war once more looming in the Ohio country, Zeisberger feared that his Christians might again be in danger. The clergyman who had once spied for the Americans now turned to the British for help. With the assistance of Elliott and McKee, he arranged for his people to move to a temporary home on the Canadian side of the Detroit River until a permanent place could be found for them. This was convenient for Elliott and McKee, who owned the property on which the Moravians were camped. The Christians were available as cheap farm labour. Simon also hired Moravians to work on his farm.

No doubt Zeisberger had unpleasant memories of the night he and his colleague, John Heckewelder, were terrorized by the "beast in human form." He soon had another reason to believe that the notorious Simon Girty was a devil sent to torment him. Simon paid his Moravian workers with rum and they got drunk on it, much to the reverend's dismay. Simon might have been having a laugh at Zeisberger's expense, but in frontier communities where cash was often in short supply, it was quite common for workers to be paid in goods. Rum and whiskey were easily tradable commodities that were practically as good as money. Simon could have argued that it wasn't his fault if his workers drank their wages. He would soon have greater concerns than Zeisberger's complaints.

Rumours reached Detroit that a big American army was assembling at Fort Washington, a new stronghold at the mouth of the Little Miami River. Native spies confirmed the rumours to be true. The mauling of General Harmar's army at the hands of "savages" had embarrassed and outraged the American government. Secretary of War Knox had ordered General Arthur St. Clair to raise a force of three thousand men to attack the Shawnees and Miamis. The principal target was a collection of Miami towns on the Wabash River.

St. Clair had only six hundred regular troops at his disposal. The bulk of his invading force would have to be made up of levies (men who had enlisted in the army for six months) and militia from Pennsylvania and Kentucky. The senior officer of the militia, and St. Clair's second-in-command, was former commissioner Richard Butler, who now enjoyed the rank of general.

The size of the army being assembled at Fort Washington gave the British and the chiefs of the confederation great cause for concern. The Americans clearly intended to drive the Natives out of the Ohio country. If they were successful, the way would be open to Detroit — and Canada!

Simon, McKee, and Elliott were dispatched to the Miami towns to distribute arms and supplies to the warriors of Little Turtle and Blue Jacket. A far-flung call to help the Shawnees and Miamis fight the invaders had been answered by warriors from all over the confederacy: Delawares, Wyandots, Ottawas, Kickapoos, Chippewas, Potawatamis, and Creeks. Brant now favoured negotiating with the Americans, so only a handful of Six Nations warriors joined the Native army on the Wabash. Spies lurking in the woods outside Fort Washington kept the chiefs informed of American activities.

In early September American advance units began construction on Fort Hamilton on the banks of the Great Miami River. Over a thousand warriors moved down to a position at the Miami Rapids, where they intended to intercept St. Clair. Simon and the other agents kept the supply line operating smoothly, and encouraged impatient warriors to stay there and wait for the coming fight.

St. Clair didn't arrive at Fort Hamilton with the main body of his army until October 1. It was already late in the season for a wilderness campaign, but the general did not move with any sense of urgency. He was certain that just the size of his force would be enough to intimidate the Natives into submitting.

St. Clair had a total of 2,700 men. However, most of them were untrained and undisciplined levies and militia. They were poorly equipped, and even the uniforms and shoes of the regular troops were of shoddy quality. Because of poor planning, difficult terrain, and bad weather, the supply line failed to maintain a sufficient flow of food and other provisions to the men. St. Clair was almost incapacitated by agonizing bouts of gout, and he did not get along well with Richard Butler. The militiamen balked at taking orders from anyone but their own elected militia officers.

Photo courtesy of the Clements Library, Ann Arbor, Michigan.

General Arthur St. Clair. His defeat at the Battle of the Wabash was the worst ever inflicted by Natives on an American army in the history of the United States.

The army began to move north from Fort Hamilton on October 4. Trailing behind the soldiers and militiamen was a long train of freight wagons accompanied by about two hundred camp followers: cooks, laundresses, prostitutes, surgeons, and even the wives and children of men in the column. St. Clair had five cannons and two mortars, but the difficulty of hauling these heavy weapons through the forest made them more of a liability than an advantage.

St. Clair's army moved slowly, with spies watching it every step of the way. In five days it advanced only twenty-five miles. Then frost came and killed the forage needed for the horses and draught animals. The cold weather turned downright miserable, and the men endured rain and hail. Cold, wet, hungry men became ill. The ranks of the militia and the levies thinned as men deserted in large numbers. Some of the deserters went all the way to Detroit, where in return for a good meal and a warm place to sleep, they told the British officers all they wanted to know about St. Clair's army. Runners carried the information to the chiefs and agents waiting at the Miami rapids.

On October 14, St. Clair halted his advance to build a rough stockade he called Fort Jefferson. He was still only about seventy-five miles from Fort Washington. Hoping to stop the rash of desertions, he had three captured deserters hanged in front of the assembled army. This demoralized the men even further.

St. Clair's army began to move forward again on October 24, but had to stop after covering just five miles because the men had no food. The supply wagons were four days behind them. Men continued to desert in spite of the threat of hanging. Some of the deserters were caught by the warriors, and taken to Simon to be questioned. In a letter to McKee that he dictated on October 28, Simon reported that deserters and other prisoners were being brought in daily. He knew just how much infantry and cavalry St. Clair had, his problems with supplies, and even how much the militiamen were being paid. Simon also told McKee, "The Indians were never in greater heart to meet their Enemy, nor more sure of success, they are determined to drive them to the Ohio, and starve their little posts by taking all their horses and cattle."

Although the British had armed and supplied the Natives, the agents had clear orders not to participate in the fighting — the Americans could regard that as an act of war by Great Britain — but the four hundred Wyandots present called on Simon to personally lead them into battle. It was an honour that he wouldn't even consider refusing. He had been raised to be a warrior, and he wasn't going to watch such an important battle from the sidelines.

On October 29, Richard Butler sent 120 men ahead of the column to chop a road through the woods for the artillery and wagons. The army resumed its advance the next day, but within forty-eight hours it had to halt again to wait for the supply train to catch up. A party of sixty Kentuckians deserted en masse.

Scouts had reported sighting warriors in the woods, but St. Clair was unconcerned. He didn't think the Natives would dare to attack his army. He was more worried that the deserters would rob the supply wagons of food and other supplies. He sent Major James Hamtramck and three hundred regulars — half of his most reliable troops — back down the road to guard the wagons.

Over the next few days the army slogged along, slowed by marshy ground, rain, snow, and St. Clair's gout. More men fell ill. On November 3, the Americans stopped in mid-afternoon near the headwaters of the Wabash River to set up camp on an island of high ground rising up from the marshes. The army had covered only six miles that day. Meanwhile, in just four days Simon and the warriors had easily travelled fifty miles and were camped no more than three miles from the Americans. By dawn the following morning, Little Turtle and Blue Jacket had their men in position. Simon was surprised to see that the Americans hadn't even bothered to fortify their camp.

On the cold, clear dawn of November 4, 1791, the main body of St. Clair's army was camped on the east bank of the Wabash River. An advance company of Kentucky militia was camped on the west bank. The men were starting fires to cook their breakfast. They had stacked their guns so they could cook and eat.

The Battle of the Wabash began when Simon and the Wyandots opened fire and then rushed the Kentuckians, taking them completely by surprise. A few of the militiamen managed to grab their guns and fire a ragged volley, but most of them panicked and ran. Some made it across the shallow river to the main camp. Their headlong flight caused confusion among the regulars and levies whom the officers were trying to get into battle lines. Amidst the chaos of shouts, war cries, and gunfire, the warriors swooped into St. Clair's main camp. Three hundred regulars formed a proper skirmishing line and fired a volley that momentarily checked the Native attack.

Little Turtle sent warriors around to outflank the regulars. Native sharpshooters began picking off officers. In the centre, the gunners loaded their cannons. There was a series of deafening blasts as the big guns sent round shot and canister screaming toward Simon and his Wyandots, who were advancing up the slope at a run. But by this time the warriors were too close for the gunners to lower their muzzles enough to be effective. The shot passed harmlessly through the tree branches above the attackers, showering them with leaves and twigs. Simon and his men answered with musket and rifle fire. Within minutes, all of the artillery crews were dead and the big guns were silenced.

With his centre on the verge of being overrun, St. Clair made a desperate attempt at a counterattack. He threw his regulars into a bayonet charge, supported by twenty-five cavalrymen. Simon and the Wyandots fell back across the river, with the troops in pursuit. Once they were in the woods, the warriors turned and annihilated the courageous but outnumbered soldiers.

By this time St. Clair's camp had been inundated. The general had several horses shot out from under him as he galloped back and forth, trying to rally his troops. When he saw some militiamen and levies hiding under wagons, St. Clair cried, "Cowards! Cowards! Cowards!"

Screams of terror filled the air as the warriors fell upon the helpless camp followers. They were tomahawked without mercy and scalped. After three hours of savage fighting, St. Clair and his surviving officers realized that their situation was hopeless. The general ordered a full retreat. The men who could still run broke through the Native encirclement and followed him down the road toward Fort Jefferson. They abandoned their supplies, their artillery, and their wounded. Small pockets of men had been cut off during the battle and couldn't join the retreat. They fought desperately for their lives, but were overwhelmed and killed.

Warriors chased the remnants of St. Clair's army down the trail, killing and scalping stragglers. They might have massacred almost all of his command if they had kept up the pursuit, but after about three miles they gave it up so they could go back to join in killing and scalping the wounded and looting the camp. They had won a great victory, and every warrior wanted his share of the plunder.

Simon walked through the battlefield in the wake of St. Clair's retreat. Gunsmoke still hung in the air, and the surrounding stench was almost overpowering. Battlefields always stank, not only with the reek of blood, but also because wounded men vomited and lost control of their bladders and bowels. There was never anything glorious about a battlefield. Nonetheless, Simon felt elated. The tribes had stood up to the biggest army the Americans had ever sent against them, and they had *won*.

All around Simon the victorious warriors were stripping the dead and mutilating the bodies. They believed that would cause the ghosts of their slain enemies to be crippled in the spirit world. They also stuffed the mouths of the dead soldiers with dirt, since land was what the Americans wanted so badly.

Then Simon saw two Shawnee warriors and another agent approach an American officer who was sitting on the ground, propped up against a tree. The man was wounded, but still alive, and in one trembling hand he held a silver plated pistol. It took Simon a moment to recognize him. Richard Butler! His old enemy from years ago in Pittsburgh! The arrogant commissioner who had forced chiefs to sign away their lands.

From the red that soaked Butler's uniform, it was evident that he had been shot in the side and was probably bleeding to death. The man who hated white "Injun lovers" even more than he hated Natives pointed his pistol at the agent and squeezed the trigger. The hammer just snapped — a misfire! Butler dropped the gun and reached for another silver plated pistol tucked into his belt. Before he could draw it, one of the Shawnees finished him with a musket shot.

As the warrior seized the dead man by the hair so he could take the scalp, Simon walked over and told the agent and the Shawnees who the American officer was. He suggested that they send Butler's scalp to Joseph Brant. Simon wanted the Mohawk chief to see what true warriors had done while he sat in comfort and safety in his home in Canada.

The Battle of the Wabash was the worst defeat ever inflicted on an American army by Natives. Of the men who had marched out of Fort Washington with St. Clair, 632 were dead or missing and 264 of those who escaped the battlefield were wounded. Only twenty-four of the regulars came out of the battle unscathed. Almost all of the camp followers were killed; just a few survivors had been taken prisoner. The Native casualties were twenty-one killed and forty wounded.

The spoils that fell to the victors were incredible: food, livestock, tents, tools, wagons, portable forges, all of St. Clair's artillery pieces, and 1,200 muskets. As a reward for his courage and leadership in the battle, the Wyandots presented Simon with three of the cannons. He expressed gratitude for the honour, but he had no way of transporting the big guns back to Malden. He had them buried and explained that he would retrieve them at a future date. Meanwhile, tucked into the sash Simon wore around his waist was a brace of silver-plated pistols.

Simon collected all the American documents he could find on bodies and in the shattered camp and bundled them up for delivery to McKee. Then he headed home to Catherine and his children. He was in Malden in time for Christmas.

Word of the disaster quickly spread to the American settlements and then to the cities in the east. Because Simon had been so conspicuous on the battlefield, the Americans believed that he had been in command of the entire Native force. Congress placed a hefty reward on his head. Whoever captured Simon Girty and brought him in alive to face an American court would be paid a bounty of five hundred guineas, plus a pension of $40 a month for life. (A guinea was a gold coin of greater value than an American dollar or a British pound.) To the average American that was a fortune, but no would-be bounty hunters ever tried to collect it. Settlers were more concerned about defending their families from the Indian raids they were sure would be coming, led by the infamous White Savage.

15

Mad Anthony

General Arthur St. Clair was obliged to resign in disgrace, but even an angry Congress and a thoroughly disappointed President Washington had to concede that responsibility for the defeat did not rest with him alone. The War Department had done a poor job of equipping and supplying his army. Moreover, Washington now realized that an army made up mostly of untrained, undisciplined militia was no match for a large force of determined warriors fighting on their home ground under very able leaders. The conquest of the Ohio country would require a large, well-trained, and properly equipped army, led by a capable commander. Filling that bill would take time.

On April 3, 1792, after considering many officers, Washington chose retired Brigadier General Anthony Wayne to build and lead the new army. Wayne, forty-seven, was vain, corpulent, a hard drinker, and a womanizer. But he was a veteran of the Revolutionary War whose aggressiveness in battle had earned him the nickname "Mad Anthony." He also had a reputation as a disciplinarian — an absolute necessity if he was to whip several thousand raw recruits into an effective fighting force.

As soon as he received his commission from President Washington, General Wayne went to Pittsburgh to start work. In order to buy him time, and in hopes of distracting the Natives from raiding, Secretary of War Knox sent six emissaries to invite the chiefs to peace talks. All six were killed! After their great victory, the chiefs weren't interested in negotiations. They wanted the Ohio River as a boundary, and nothing less. Agents like Simon and McKee supported this stand.

The Natives considered all Americans on the north side of the Ohio to be trespassers, so they raided, even as the British in Detroit urged them to show "moderation," meaning that they should refrain from killing women and children, and torturing captives. On July 21, Simon was in Blue Jacket's Town at the confluence of the Maumee and Auglaize rivers, a spot known as The Glaize. There he met eleven-year-old Oliver Spence, whom Shawnee warriors had captured two weeks earlier. The boy was in the care of an elderly widow who took him to Blue Jacket's lodge to join the chief and Simon for supper. Years later, Spence provided a description of Simon.

> Girty wore an Indian outfit, but without ornament, upon this occasion; and his silk handkerchief, while it supplied the place of a hat, hid the unsightly scar in his forehead, caused by the wound which ... was given him by Captain Joseph Brant. On each side, in his belt, was

stuck a silver-mounted pistol, and at his left hung a short, broad dirk, serving occasionally the uses of a knife.

Four major councils were held at The Glaize during the summer of 1792. Simon was the only white man allowed to attend. Henry Knox would later write in a letter reporting to President Washington on the meetings:

> He (an American agent) was informed by the chiefs of the Six Nations, that, at the council of the hostile Indians, which was numerous, but the numbers not specified, no other white person was admitted but Simon Girty, whom they consider as one of themselves.

The chiefs were aware that even though the American government was calling for peace talks, General Wayne was at Pittsburgh building an army. The representatives of twenty-eight tribes were sharply divided on how to meet this threat. Joseph Brant wasn't present, but the Iroquois Chief Red Jacket spoke for the tribes who favoured making concessions to the Americans. The Miamis, Shawnees, Wyandots, Ottawas, and Potawatomis insisted on fighting if the Americans refused to recognize the Ohio as the boundary. They accused Red Jacket of being an agent for the Americans.

After weeks of debate and argument, all of the chiefs finally agreed on a letter to be sent to Congress via Joseph Brant. He would deliver the message to the American agent for the Six Nations. The chiefs said that they were willing to meet representatives of the United States for peace talks, but they flatly stated that there could be no peace as long as American forts remained on the north side of the Ohio.

On November 6, Little Turtle and Blue Jacket led a hundred warriors in an attack on a Kentucky brigade camped outside Fort St. Clair. After a sharp fight, most of the Kentuckians retreated into the fort. They had six men killed, five wounded, and four missing. Of the one hundred pack horses the Kentuckians had been guarding, twenty-six were killed and ten injured. The warriors made off with the rest. Mad Anthony wanted to retaliate, but he wasn't ready ... yet!

There is evidence that at about this time, Simon was in Pittsburgh on yet another spy mission. This time he was disguised as an old French Canadian. While there is no record that Simon learned to speak French, he had been in the company of French Canadians for many years, in Detroit and on the trail. Given his gift for learning languages easily, it's quite possible that he picked up enough French to convincingly pass himself off in the American community as a French Canadian who spoke broken English. According to Simon's own account, he spent an evening in a Pittsburgh tavern that was popular with soldiers and officers. Just a few feet away from the "old Frenchman" who wore a battered hat to hide a giveaway scar was Mad Anthony Wayne himself!

Knox's reply to the confederation reached The Glaize in February 1793. Simon was invited to join the chiefs in discussing what the Secretary of War had to say. Knox was pleased that the chiefs were willing to discuss peace, and said that American delegates would meet them in the summer at the Miami Rapids. He said that in the meantime the chiefs must stop their warriors from raiding. His message said nothing about the Ohio River or the removal of the forts.

General "Mad Anthony" Wayne. The Revolutionary War veteran realized that undisciplined militia was no match for determined warriors with able leaders. His well-trained army defeated the confederated tribes at the Battle of Fallen Timbers.

The chiefs were uncertain about this response and wondered if Brant had given the Americans their message in its entirety. They sent Knox another message, in which they said that it seemed that he wanted war. They demanded that the meeting take place at Sandusky, and nowhere else. As a show of good faith, they agreed to stop raiding. Meanwhile, they sent a separate message to Brant, requesting that he and other Six Nations representatives come to The Glaize for talks before the summer council with the Americans.

At the end of February a reply came from Knox. The American delegates would meet the chiefs at Sandusky on the first of June. The chiefs were pleased with this show of compromise, but not happy that Knox had again neglected to say anything about the Ohio or the forts.

In March McKee received a letter from Brant. He and the other Six Nations leaders, including the aging Guyasuta, felt that the only way to have peace with the Americans was to move the boundary from the Ohio to the Muskingum River. Brant didn't think it was realistic to expect the Americans would give up the forts and settlements they already had north of the Ohio. It would be better, he said, for the western tribes to give up that territory and withdraw to the east side of the Muskingum.

This message showed a major split in the confederation. McKee, Elliott, and Simon might have reluctantly admitted to themselves that Brant was right. But they had orders from John Graves Simcoe, the Lieutenant Governor of Upper Canada, to encourage the Shawnee and Miami chiefs to insist on the Ohio River boundary.

Meanwhile, at a military post called Legionville twenty-one miles south of Pittsburgh, General Wayne's army was taking shape. Mad Anthony drilled his troops relentlessly. They learned to move fast, form battle lines quickly, and fire precision volleys as they advanced in formation. His riflemen were armed with the latest guns and were trained to be marksmen. His infantry had a new form of ammunition for their muskets — a paper cartridge that allowed fast, easy reloading. Each cartridge contained a charge of gunpowder and a load of large and small bullets called "buck and ball" that ripped flesh and bone to shreds.

Wayne gave special attention to training his infantry in the bayonet charge. Once a battle came to close quarters, the infantryman's main weapon was the long bayonet at the end of his musket. In hand-to-hand combat it was more deadly than a tomahawk. By late April, Wayne was ready to move his army to Fort Washington, outside the little settlement of Cincinnati.

In mid-May three American delegates arrived at Niagara: Benjamin Lincoln, Beverley Randolph, and Timothy Pickering. One of their party was John Heckewelder, Simon's old adversary. John Graves Simcoe welcomed them heartily, and even held a ball in their honour. Simcoe was so hospitable and charming that the Americans let their guard down and revealed a lot of information about their mission that they would have been well advised to keep to themselves. Simcoe was particularly disturbed to learn for the first time that a state of war had existed between Britain and France since February.

This news was of vital importance. If the United States decided to form an alliance with France, the British would need the Native confederation to be strong. Their territory was the buffer zone between the Americans and Upper Canada. Simcoe rushed this information to McKee at The Glaize by secret messenger. McKee and Simon urged the chiefs to settle their differences. In Detroit, Elliott distributed guns and ammunition to visiting warriors.

Over the next few weeks, Simon was again obliged to work with Joseph Brant as an agent and interpreter. Brant was the diplomatic go-between in a series of meetings leading up to the planned big council at Sandusky. Simon noted that whether Brant was talking to the Americans or the western chiefs, he avoided the issue of the Ohio River boundary. As much as Simon disliked Brant, he undoubtedly understood that the Mohawk chief was walking on a thin edge as he tried to bring the two sides to a compromise and avoid another war. But the chiefs who were most hostile to the Americans were suspicious of Brant.

During a meeting at The Glaize on July 26, the inter-tribal tension finally snapped. The Shawnees and Miamis angrily declared that they wanted the Ohio River boundary and would fight for it if necessary. They had prepared a message to that effect to be sent to the Americans, and they wanted all of the confederation chiefs to agree to it. Brant refused. The Ottawas, Chippewas and Potawatomies sided with him.

By this time the American delegates were guests in Matthew Elliott's house near Malden, wondering when, or *if*, they would go on to Sandusky. To their surprise, the Natives came to them. Late in July more than thirty confederation representatives arrived at Bois Blanc Island in the Detroit River, just across from Elliott's farm. Brant was not with them. Instead, their spokesman was the Wyandot chief Sa-wagh-da-wunk. Simon was their principal interpreter.

On July 30 the delegates for the two sides met at Elliott's farm. According to Heckewelder, Simon showed his contempt for the Americans by "wearing a quill or long feather run through the under part of his nose cross ways." With Simon translating, Sa-wagh-da-wunk greeted the Americans and then got right down to business. He handed them the letter that demanded a clear answer to a clear question. Were the American delegates authorized by their government to establish the Ohio River as the permanent boundary between the United States and the western tribes?

The Americans were surprised by this, but noted that Brant's signature wasn't on the document. They didn't respond until the next day. Timothy Pickering said that the forts and settlements north of the Ohio were there by right of treaty, and removing them would be too expensive. He wanted the chiefs to confirm the Treaty of Fort Harmar. Pickering promised that the tribes would be paid for the lands they had given up, and that he and his colleagues were authorized to negotiate a new, permanent boundary that the United States would respect.

Sa-wagh-da-wunk had none of Brant's diplomatic skills. Brant might have worked out a compromise that would have at least temporarily satisfied the Americans without causing the chiefs to lose face. But speaking through Simon, Sa-wagh-da-wunk told the Americans, "You have your houses and people on our land. We cannot give up our land. You may return whence you came and tell Washington." Sa-wagh-da-wunk had in effect bluntly told the Americans, "Go home!"

Elliott quickly interrupted and said that Simon had made a mistake in translating. He hastily conferred with Simon, Sa-wagh-da-wunk, and the other chiefs. Then Simon delivered a "corrected" translation.

"We wish you to remain here for an answer from us ... we have your speech in our hearts and shall consult with our head warriors."

The chiefs returned to The Glaize where Brant once again tried to convince them to compromise, but the Shawnees, Miamis and their allies were unmovable. They said they'd had enough of empty American promises. With McKee's help, they composed a formal letter to the American delegates. It said that the United States had no right to their country. Money was of no value to them — the American government could give it to the poor settlers who would have to abandon their farms when they got off Native land. The American delegates took the letter as a declaration of war. They sent a quick message to General Wayne: "We did not effect a peace."

It was now near the end of summer and Mad Anthony wanted to move against the tribes immediately. But he didn't have sufficient provisions, and epidemics of smallpox and influenza swept through his army. He advanced only seven miles from Fort Jefferson and built a new post, Fort Greenville.

When McKee learned that the Americans were on the move, he sent Simon to spy on them. Simon carried out the mission, even though the U.S. government had placed a new bounty of $1,000 on his head. He reported back that Wayne's army appeared to have gone into winter camp and probably wouldn't march until the spring. Simon then went home to spend the winter with his family.

Mad Anthony didn't intend to spend the whole winter sitting still. On Christmas Eve he set out with eight companies of infantry for the site of St. Clair's defeat. He put his men to work burying the bones of the slain soldiers and building another post, Fort Recovery. He also found the three buried cannons the Wyandots had awarded to Simon. Wayne went back to Fort Greenville, leaving a garrison of two hundred in Fort Recovery.

The British in Canada were sure that within a year they would be at war with the United States. Governor General Sir Guy Carlton in Quebec gave John Graves Simcoe orders to build a new military post, Fort Miamis, on the Maumee River and garrison it with regular soldiers from Detroit. This was a blatant violation of the peace treaty between Great Britain and the United States, but Carlton had decided that in the event of war he had to strengthen the British hold on the West and prove to the Natives that Britain was still their ally.

Throughout the spring of 1794, as Fort Miamis was being constructed, Simon, McKee, and Elliott were busy encouraging the tribes to stay united. They promised arms and provisions and hinted that if war broke out between Britain and the United States, British troops and Canadian militia would again fight side-by-side with the warriors. They spread the message that The Glaize was the assembly point.

Once again, hundreds of warriors from all of the confederated tribes — except the Iroquois — answered the call: Shawnees, Delawares, Miamis, Ottawas, Chippewas, Wyandots, and Potawatomies. By mid-June, Little Turtle and Blue Jacket had a force of over 1,200 men. There were also British traders and Canadian frontiersmen in the vicinity, whom the chiefs declared would have to fight alongside the warriors. These whites were obliged to wear Native dress so they wouldn't be mistaken for the enemy during the battle.

But in spite of its numbers, this Native army had problems. McKee and Elliott had been unable to procure enough arms and food for so many men. Ten percent of the warriors had no guns and carried only their traditional weapons. Hunters had to go out everyday in search of game. Old inter-tribal disputes flared up, undermining unity. The warriors of the Ohio country were especially incensed to learn that a band of Lakes warriors from Mackinaw and Saginaw had behaved like marauders on their journey south, pillaging the villages of their allies and raping the women.

Simon, McKee, and Elliott used all of their influence to try to hold the warrior army together, but the chiefs were unable to agree on anything. The Shawnees and Miamis had made a successful raid on Wayne's supply lines, killing forty of his soldiers and losing only one warrior. They wanted to continue this strategy, and McKee agreed. But the Lake warriors — the Ottawas, Chippewas, and Potawatomies — argued for an attack on Fort Recovery.

While the chiefs squabbled for days over what to do, their scouts clashed with a party of Chickasaws who were scouting for the Americans. One Chickasaw was killed, but the rest escaped. Now Little Turtle and Blue Jacket knew that Mad Anthony was aware of their position and would be on his guard. Against McKee's advice, they gave in to the Lake chiefs and decided to attack Fort Recovery.

Simon was with the Natives who struck the fort on the morning of June 30. Outside the walls was a supply train of 360 pack horses guarded by 140 soldiers. In the sudden attack the warriors killed forty men and captured three hundred horses. Simon considered this a success, and agreed with Little Turtle and Blue Jacket, who wanted to withdraw and concentrate on harassing Wayne's supply lines.

However, the Lakes chiefs were so taken with the easy victory that they insisted on a full assault against the fort. The attack was a disaster! The warriors charged across the open ground around the walls and were mowed down by rifle and cannon fire. During the battle, Ohio warriors shot Lakes warriors in the back in revenge for the raping of their women.

The Natives withdrew, using the captured horses to carry away their many dead and wounded. Little Turtle and Blue Jacket blamed the Lakes chiefs for turning a victory into defeat.

Those chiefs in turn accused the Shawnees of firing on their warriors from behind. With morale in shreds and all sense of unity gone, hundreds of Ottawas and Chippewas headed for home.

The warrior army had been infiltrated by General Wayne's Native spies. They slipped away and reported the disintegration of Little Turtle's fighting force. From them Wayne also learned that the enemy was so short of food, they had slaughtered and eaten many of the captured horses. Most significant to Mad Anthony was the information that although Simon Girty and a handful of Canadians disguised as Natives had participated in the fighting, only a couple of British officers (McKee and Elliott) were present, and they had stayed well to the rear. This told Wayne that the British didn't want to be seen actually fighting with the Natives. He was now sure that while Little Turtle might get some help from Canadian militia, they'd get none from the British troops in Fort Miamis.

Simon, McKee, and Elliott now had the daunting task of mending the damage that the fiasco at Fort Recovery had done to the confederation. They pointed out to the disgruntled chiefs that Fort Miamis was being well supplied with guns, ammunition, and food. They couldn't directly promise that the British army would assist the warriors with soldiers and cannons, but they were under orders to give the chiefs the impression that the British were ready to fully support them on the battlefield.

Simon knew that he and his fellow agents were deceiving the chiefs, and he didn't like it. But he also knew that if the warriors didn't stop General Wayne they would lose all of the Ohio country. Therefore he told the chiefs that if they could put their differences aside and hold together, at least for a little while, they might still defeat the Americans. Wayne's army would have to come out into the open to fight them, and wouldn't be protected by the walls of a fort. Hadn't the tribes beaten the Americans time and time again in open battles? This argument struck home, and hundreds of warriors returned to The Glaize. The Native army swelled to 1,200 men, all eager to fight.

On the grey, drizzly morning of August 20, the American army stood poised for battle at a place called Fallen Timbers, about five miles south of Fort Miamis. The chiefs had decided that The Glaize was too vulnerable, so they had withdrawn to this thickly wooded position where a tangle of trees felled by a tornado formed a natural defensive works. It also put them within easy reach of Fort Miamis, which had been reinforced with redcoat troops from Detroit.

Raiders had harassed Wayne's scouting patrols, but the bulk of the confederation army was concentrated at Fallen Timbers. With them were a hundred Canadian militiamen commanded by Simon's old comrade-in-arms, Colonel William Caldwell. The Canadians were dressed and painted like Natives.

General Wayne had 2,200 well-trained regular troops and 1,500 Kentucky militiamen, many of them mounted. Behind his army lay a string of forts he had constructed during his advance into enemy territory. Along the way he had burned abandoned villages and cornfields.

Thanks to General Wayne's efficiency, his troops were well fed. The Natives opposing them were not. That morning, Simon, McKee, and Elliott were at Fort Miamis trying to arrange distribution of food to the hundreds of refugee women and children camped outside the walls. The warriors on the front line at Fallen Timbers had eaten little or nothing for three days. Several hundred of them had gone to the fort to get food for themselves and their comrades. Only half of the warrior force was in position when

Mad Anthony launched his attack. One of them was the young Shawnee, Tecumseh.

Mounted Kentucky militia charged the Native position and were met with a volley of musket fire and arrows. The horsemen discharged their rifles, and then appeared to fall back in panic. Many of the warriors were veterans of Harmar's and St. Clair's defeats, and they sensed another easy victory. They rushed out to pursue the Kentuckians, which was exactly what General Wayne had expected they'd do.

As the warriors chased the "fleeing" Kentuckians, they suddenly ran into Wayne's disciplined regulars. The Native counterattack faltered before volleys of buck-and-ball and cannon fire. Then the American troops advanced in a series of bayonet charges that sent the warriors reeling backwards so quickly they couldn't even stop to reload their guns. The warriors fell back into the maze of Fallen Timbers, with the soldiers right on their heels. There, amidst the tangles of uprooted trees, the fighting was up close and bloody — tomahawk against bayonet. The American line was longer than the Native line, and the soldiers turned to outflank the warriors. Caldwell and his Canadians tried to prevent the flanking manoeuvre. They fought bravely, but they were outnumbered. The best they could do was provide a rearguard covering fire for the fleeing warriors.

Simon didn't get into the battle at all. He was riding back from Fort Miamis with McKee and Elliott when he heard gunfire and then saw warriors in full flight burst from the trees and run for the fort. Simon could do nothing but watch. The battle was clearly lost, and McKee ordered him not to interfere.

The final betrayal came when the warriors reached the fort. The chiefs shouted for the British to come out and help them fight the Americans. Why were the redcoat soldiers hiding in the fort? Why weren't they loading their cannons to blast the enemy, who would come racing out of the trees at any moment, charging with their bayonets? The fort's commander, Major William Campbell, looked down from a rampart and said, "My orders instruct me to do nothing more than safeguard the integrity of this fort."

Then the Natives banged on the gates and demanded to at least be allowed in for protection, but the gates remained closed. Confused, disillusioned, enraged, the Natives fled again, all the way to Swan Creek, near the mouth of the Maumee River.

That night, Simon, McKee, and Elliott took their lives in their hands when they went not to the safety of the fort, but to Swan Creek. McKee and Elliott wanted to explain that Major Campbell was acting under orders and couldn't risk touching off a war with the United States. Simon just wanted to share the burden of defeat with his fellow warriors. The chiefs might have felt fully justified in taking out their anger at the British treachery on the three white men, but they knew that with their villages and cornfields in ashes, the people were going to rely on British help to get through the coming winter.

16

An Old Warrior Without a War

After his victory at Fallen Timbers, Mad Anthony could have taken Fort Miamis by storm and then marched on Detroit. Instead, he withdrew to Fort Greenville to await the Native peace delegates he knew would be coming. He did, however, burn down McKee's storehouse at Roche de Bout.

Simon and Elliott spent most of the winter at Swan Creek, doing whatever they could to assist the five thousand homeless and hungry refugees. McKee went to Detroit to plead for provisions and was able to procure an insufficient supply of pork and flour. In December, on orders from Detroit, Simon carried out one last spy mission. He went to Fort Greenville to see what General Wayne was doing, and reported that the American army was settled in for the winter.

John Graves Simcoe, Joseph Brant, McKee, Elliott, and Simon all tried to convince the confederation chiefs to resume the war against the Americans in the spring of 1795. But Fallen

Timbers had crushed their spirits. The betrayal at Fort Miamis had left them with a deep and bitter mistrust of the British.

In August 1795, almost a hundred chiefs representing a dozen tribes from the Ohio country and the Great Lakes region met General Wayne at Greenville and signed the treaties he had ready and waiting. The land the tribes were forced to cede to the Americans included all of the present states of Illinois, Michigan, and Wisconsin, most of southern and eastern Ohio, most of Indiana, and all of Minnesota east of the Mississippi River. A small slice of the Ohio country was left to the Natives, but in time even that would be taken away.

General Wayne's victory also meant that the British had to finally give up their western posts, including Detroit. On July 7, 1796, Simon made his dramatic escape from the soldiers who had come to take possession of the town. Safe on the Canadian side of the river, and with his farm and family awaiting him, Simon might have looked forward to a quiet and comfortable old age after so many years of conflict and adventure. But peace and quiet would always be strangers to Simon Girty.

Simon was fifty-five years old, a senior citizen in a time and place where the average life expectancy was thirty-five. He was strong and active, and generally in robust health. His one physical problem was the old head wound that still caused him paralyzing headaches. Simon had his farm and he was retired from the British Indian Department on a pension. From time to time he was summoned to work as an interpreter at Fort Malden, which the British had built near his home.

However, the life of a gentleman farmer had never held much appeal for Simon. All his adult life he'd been a man of action and he'd had a cause to fight for. Now he was an old warrior with no more battles to fight — no more bold missions into enemy territory. He had also lost some old friends. In 1794 his fellow warriors Captain Pipe and Half King had died. The following year Guyasuta died. The once great Seneca chief had been reduced to a drunken beggar. Then on February 26, 1796, Simon's brother George died in a Delaware community not far from Gosfield, Upper Canada.

James Girty lived with his family on a farm at Gosfield, so he and Simon could visit each other frequently. But Thomas and John Turner still lived near Pittsburgh, which was now more than ever forbidden territory for Simon. When Simon impulsively decided that he had to see them again, it was probably as much out of the need to dare fate one more time. The visit almost ended in disaster.

Simon disguised himself so he wouldn't be recognized by Pittsburgh residents who knew him. However, while he was at John's Squirrel Hill farm, neighbours became suspicious of the unfamiliar horse and the strange old man they'd seen on the property. A rumour spread that John Turner's outlaw half-brother was in the house. When Simon and John saw a party of men approach the house, Simon hid in a closet. He was so fearful of being discovered that he wrapped his silver watch in a sock and stuffed it in his pocket so the unwelcome visitors wouldn't hear it ticking.

John convinced his neighbours that they were on a wild goose chase, and the men left. Then he had to tell Simon not to come to his home again because of the danger to his family. Simon got on his horse and headed back to Upper Canada, probably without stopping to visit Thomas. He would still keep up correspondence with his American brothers, and Simon and John mentioned each other's children in their wills.

On October 20, 1796, Catherine gave birth to another son, named Bredon Prideaux. Sadly, the child was born into an unhappy household. Simon had always enjoyed drinking with his friends, but he had never been a drunkard who let liquor interfere with his work. Now that he was retired and feeling like a man without purpose, he drank more. He became moody. According to some accounts he was abusive to Catherine, but there seems to be little evidence to substantiate these claims. Nonetheless, Simon's drinking became prodigious. Sometimes he would sit in a tavern, swilling rum with his friends and reliving the old days. At other times, he would get on his horse and gallop from one tavern to another, drinking in the saddle, whooping like a warrior in battle and scattering groups of startled people. Some people winked at Simon's incorrigible behaviour, but Catherine finally lost all patience with him.

Early in 1798, Catherine left Simon and went to live with her brother Peter in Gosfield. She took eighteen-month-old Prideaux with her. The rest of the children stayed with their father.

In January 1799, Simon lost another friend when his long-time colleague Alexander McKee fell ill and died. McKee's son Thomas was appointed his successor as senior British Indian Department agent. Matthew Elliott had been dismissed for embezzlement.

Sometime around 1800, Simon broke his right leg or ankle in a fall. The fracture never healed properly, and for the rest of his days he walked with a limp. Thereafter, Simon went almost everywhere on horseback. He carried a stout walking stick to aid him when he was on foot.

In spite of Simon's heavy drinking, Thomas McKee regularly called on his services as an interpreter. Simon also increased his land holdings. Even when he was well into his cups, he was noted for his gentlemanly behaviour toward women. Simon was on good terms with his brother-in-law Peter Malott, and it may have been through him that Simon and Catherine gradually began to repair the rift between them. But she was not yet willing to return to the farm at Malden.

On November 24, 1807, Joseph Brant died at his home in Burlington at the western end of Lake Ontario. Simon and the great Mohawk chief had never really been friends, but necessity had made them colleagues through very turbulent times. Simon might well have mourned Brant's death as the loss of yet another link with his past.

By this time both of Simon's daughters were married and living in homes of their own. Only his son Thomas remained at the homestead with him. When Thomas married in 1809, he and his new wife, Monica, stayed at the farm with Simon. In addition to being a cripple and suffering more frequently from debilitating headaches, the aging warrior was going blind. Simon's failing eyesight might have been caused by age, cataracts, or his old head wound.

In 1812, war broke out between Great Britain and the United States. Upper Canada lay exposed to invasion. The British once again sought an alliance with the Natives. The Indian Department hired several interpreters, including James Girty, but Simon was passed over as "incapable of doing anything." This decision might have been due to Simon's almost daily intoxication or his growing blindness. However, one man felt that old Simon Girty might still have some sound advice on fighting the Americans. Simon had several visits from Tecumseh, the Shawnee chief who had taken up Brant's cause of uniting the tribes into a confederation.

The war brought grief to the Girty family. In the summer of 1812, following one of the skirmishes that preceded the capture of Detroit by General Isaac Brock and Tecumseh, Ensign

Thomas Girty of the Essex Militia died after carrying a wounded Canadian officer to safety. The cause of death was either "over-exertion," or a fever. Two months later Monica gave birth to a baby girl.

Simon might have visited Detroit when it was again in British hands, but in 1813, with the defeat of the British fleet on Lake Erie, the western part of Upper Canada was once more open to attack. With the British army preparing to abandon Fort Malden and withdraw to Niagara, Matthew Elliott, who had also lost a son in the war, urged Simon to go with him to Burlington where they could stay with Brant's people until it was safe to return home. Elliott and Simon had no doubts about what would happen if they fell into American hands.

When the Americans landed on the Canadian shore, Kentucky militiamen sought out Elliott's home. They destroyed the house and furniture, as well as the barn, storehouses and fences. According to one account, they then went to Simon's house and were about to burn it down over Monica's head. They were stopped by a big frontiersman — Simon Kenton! Simon Girty's old friend was with the Kentucky militia, and had hoped that he might once again see the man who had saved his life.

On October 5, 1813, Tecumseh was killed in the Battle of Moraviantown. It was later reported in the United States that Simon Girty was also slain in that battle, "cut to pieces" by mounted Kentuckians. Actually, Simon was at Burlington, where he stayed for the duration of the war. The Mohawks treated him as they would one of their own revered elders. While Simon was content to once again be living among Natives, it now seemed that death was always lurking nearby. On May 7, 1814, Matthew Elliott died. Simon was the only one left of the infamous trio that had fled Pittsburgh so many years before.

The War of 1812 officially ended on December 24, 1814, with the signing of the Treaty of Ghent (now in Belgium), though it took almost three months for the news to reach Canada. The American attempt to conquer Canada had been a total failure, and not a single American soldier remained on Canadian soil. But Simon stayed with the Mohawks until the summer of 1816.

When Simon finally returned home, he was completely blind. Catherine went back to him so she could take care of him. Age and infirmities had subdued his wild nature, and he was no longer drinking heavily. Still, he liked to ride into Amherstburg and have a quiet drink at his daughter Anne and her husband Peter Govereau's tavern. His blindness didn't prevent him from travelling back and forth, because his horse knew the way. Anne took pride in telling strangers who stopped at the inn that the blind old man sitting at a table in a corner was her father, Simon Girty. Whereupon the stranger would reply: "And to think that they are trying to make such a villain of him!"

On April 17, 1817, James Girty died at his home in Gosfield. Now Simon was the last of the "Injun Girtys." He would soon follow George and James.

On February 15, 1818, Simon became ill and was confined to his bed. He was seventy-seven years old, and it soon became evident that he was in his last hours. Joining Simon's family praying at his bedside were old Native warriors who added their own traditional prayers. Simon died on the morning of February 18, while a blizzard howled outside. On February 20, an honour guard from Fort Malden carried his casket through deep snow to a grave site on his property. They lowered the casket into a shallow hole that had been hacked out of the frozen ground, and then fired a salute over it. Simon Girty was dead, but the legend of the White Savage would live on.

Epilogue

The newly independent Americans needed heroes to help define who they were. Obvious candidates for the mantle of immortality were such leaders as George Washington and Thomas Jefferson. They also lionized a host of other persons who, while they did indeed contribute to the struggle for independence, their deeds were nonetheless over-glorified in song and story until facts became lost in myth. Paul Revere didn't actually complete the ride that was immortalized in verse by Henry Wadsworth Longfellow. Nathan Hale never actually said, "I only regret that I have but one life to lose for my country," before he was hanged for spying. Daniel Boone was just one of many colourful, adventurous frontiersmen. Yet, all of these people were enshrined as American heroes.

Heroes must have foes to vanquish, and the more evil the foe, the more noble the hero. For American Patriots, the foe was, of course, the British; haughty, arrogant Redcoats trying to impose the unpopular rule of a tyrannical king. Then there were the Tories; colonists whom the Patriots reviled as traitors because they were loyal to the king. A popular saying went, "A Tory is a creature with its head in England, its body in America, and a neck which ought to be stretched."

Finally, there were the Natives. The Americans saw them as savages who stood in the way of brave pioneers like Daniel Boone who were civilizing the wilderness. They considered the alliance of the British with the Natives immoral because, as one nineteenth century American historian put it, "The Indians, led by British officers, were far more to be dreaded than when left to their own cunning, which was often childish."

In Simon Girty, the myth-makers had the perfect villain. He was a British agent–Tory traitor–Indian renegade all wrapped up in one evil hide. There was no crime he wouldn't commit, no level of depravity to which he wouldn't stoop. The following is just a small selection of observations made by American historians about Simon Girty.

> The notorious renegado, Simon Girty ... became one of the most cruel and inveterate foes to the whites. Through his instigation, it is well known that many prisoners were burnt at the stake, who might otherwise have been adopted into some Indian family, and their lives saved.
>
> S.P. Hildreth, *The First American Frontier.*

> ... a vile renegade by the name of Girty, not merely sustained, but encouraged the Indian in all his cruelty. He was a Tory, and one of the

bitterest foes of the white man. His life was one of wretched barbarities ... by his conduct he compromised, every hour, his employers, and caused the war of the Revolution to put on features of horror that, with all its evil, do not belong to the struggles of civilized nations.

W.H. Bogart, *Daniel Boone and the Hunters of Kentucky.*

... Simon Girty, of evil fame, whom the whole West grew to loathe, with bitter hatred, as "the white renegade." He was the son of a vicious Irish trader who was killed by the Indians.

Theodore Roosevelt, *The Winning of the West.*

If supposedly legitimate historians present Girty as a fiend, it naturally follows that writers of romantic fiction set in frontier America have found him to be a made-to-order villain. In *The Spirit of the Border*, novelist Zane Grey actually makes Simon and his brother James (known in the story as Buzzard Jim) responsible for the Moravian Massacre. *Bridal Journey*, by Dale Van Every, has Simon enter the story dragging a white youth who is a gift for the Natives to burn. He tells a shocked British officer, "When you want Indians to hanker fur war, it's allus best to let 'em work theyselves up good. And nothin' slaps the ol' pepper to 'em like givin' 'em a captive to burn."

Stephen Vincent Benet's classic short story, "The Devil and Daniel Webster," features Girty as one of Satan's Jury of the

Damned, who must sit in judgment of a man who has sold his soul for a year of prosperity. He is described as "Simon Girty, the renegade, who saw white men burned at the stake, and whooped with the Indians to see them burn. His eyes were green like a catamount's, and the stains on his hunting shirt did not come from the blood of the deer."

In the 1936 movie *Daniel Boone*, which featured a very popular actor named George O'Brien in the lead role, Simon Girty is the hero's dastardly antagonist. He is played by John Carradine, an actor best known for portraying villains. While Boone wears the iconic coonskin cap, the evil Girty wears a hat made of skunk skin. In the climactic fight at the end of the movie, Boone kills Girty.

Clips from *Daniel Boone* and from *Daniel Boone: Trailblazer*, another movie in which Simon Girty is the heavy, are shown in *Simon Girty: Crossing Over*. This documentary film explores Simon's life through visits to significant historic sites, illustrations, and interviews with historians and descendants of Simon and his contemporaries. Anne Marie Goodfellow, the documentary's producer, is Simon Girty's five-time great-grandaughter.

American novelists such as Lewis Owen (*The Indian Lover*) and Alan W. Eckert (*The Frontiersmen*) have presented Girty in a much more positive light and as a more three dimensional character. Eckert's works are, in fact, authentic historical accounts with some invented dialogue. In the War of 1812 novel *The Canadian Brothers*, by John Richardson, Canada's first novelist, the character Sampson Gattrie is directly based on Simon Girty, whom Richardson knew personally. Gattrie is an old man with a colourful past who drinks "oceans of whiskey," gallops around the country on his horse Silvertail, and tries to apprehend two escaped American prisoners of war.

Girty, by Richard Taylor, is a very artistic treatment of Simon's story. It is, in the author's words, "a collage of historical materials, including diaries, Indian captivities, travel accounts, guides, and biographies; a reconstruction of fragments, some heavily biased, which tell only part of the story. Girty himself tells the rest through a series of interior monologues divided between prose narratives and poems." *Wilderness*, by Timothy Truman, is a two-part graphic novel that gives a visually dramatic account of Simon's story.

In 1995 the United Empire Loyalists of Canada paid tribute to Simon Girty's memory with a historic plaque at the site of his homestead in Malden, Ontario. The Six Nations recognize him as an "Indian Patriot." But Girty is still not as well remembered in Canada as Joseph Brant and Tecumseh. Encyclopedia entries under his name are still riddled with errors.

In 1932, Francis X. Chauvin addressed the descendants of Simon Girty at a reunion in Kingsville, Ontario. He concluded his discourse on their ancestor with a poem, apparently of his own composition. The literary merit may be suspect, but the spirit is appropriate.

> Oh, great-souled chief, so long maligned
> By bold calumniators;
> The world shall not be always blind,
> Nor all men be thy haters.
> If ever on the field of blood,
> Man's valor merits glory,
> Then Girty's name and Girty's fame
> Shall shine in song and story.

Chronology of
Simon Girty(1741–1818)

Girty and His Times

Canada and the World

Circa 1730
Simon Girty Sr. of Ireland arrives in North America, probably at Philadelphia.

1730
The Mississaugas drive the Senecas south of Lake Erie.

1731
The La Verendrye family of explorers organize expeditions beyond Lake Winnipeg.

1732
Benjamin Franklin's *Poor Richard's Almanac* is published.

1737
The north shore road from Quebec City to Montreal opens.

The slave revolt is crushed in South Carolina.

1739
Thomas Girty (brother) born to Simon Girty Sr. and Mary Girty (*née* Newton).

Girty and His Times	*Canada and the World*
	1740 War of Austrian Succession begins.
1741 Simon Girty is born on November 14, near Harrisburg, Pennsylvania.	
1743 James Girty (brother) is born in February.	**1743** Louis Joseph de la Verendrye is the first European to see the Rocky Mountains.
	1745 The British army from New England captures Louisbourg on Ile Royale (Cape Breton Island).
1746 George Girty (brother) is born on March 8.	
	1748 The Treaty of Aix-la-Chapelle returns Louisbourg to France.
1749 Simon Girty Sr. and fellow traders illegally establish a post at Sherman's Creek in Native territory.	**1749** Halifax, Nova Scotia, is founded.
1750 May: Colonial authorities evict Simon Girty Sr. and companions from Sherman's Creek and burn down the post. Girty Sr. is fined.	**1750** Composer Johann Sebastian Bach dies following eye surgery.

Girty and His Times

Canada and the World

November: Simon Girty Sr. is killed in a quarrel with a man named Samuel Saunders, who is subsequently convicted of manslaughter and sent to prison.

The slave trade from Africa to the West Indies and North America reaches average of 60,000 people a year.

1751
February: Thomas McKee legally takes possession of Girty family property as payment for outstanding debts.

1751
Voltaire publishes *The Age of Louis XIV*.

Indonesians rebel against Dutch colonial rule.

1752
Canada's first newspaper, the *Halifax Gazette*, is published.

1753
Mary Girty marries John Turner. The family moves to Turner's farm on Penn's Creek in the Buffalo Valley.

1753
Scottish physician James Lind declares that citrus fruit cures scurvy.

1754
The Seven Years' War begins.

1754
Jean Jacques Rousseau's *Discourse on the Origins of Inequality* is published.

1755
John Turner Jr. (half-brother) is born in February.

July 9: French, Canadians, and Natives defeat the British army of General Edward Braddock as it advances on the French post, Fort Duquesne. Braddock is

1755
The British expel the Acadians.

An earthquake and tsunami destroy Lisbon, Portugal. An estimated 100,000 people are killed.

Girty and His Times	*Canada and the World*

killed, and George Washington and Daniel Boone are among the survivors.

1756
July: The entire Girty-Turner family is captured when Fort Granville falls to a French and Native force. John Turner is tortured to death. Thomas eventually escapes, but the rest of the family is dispersed. Mary, James, and the baby John Turner Jr. go to the Shawnees; George to the Delawares; and Simon to the Senecas.

September/October: In a Seneca town on the south shore of Lake Erie, Simon successfully runs the gauntlet and is adopted into the tribe. He begins his education as a warrior, orator, and interpreter. His mentor is probably Chief Guyasuta.

1756
The Marquis de Montcalm arrives in Quebec and quickly captures Fort Oswego.

The conflict in Calcutta between the British East India Company and the Mughal Prince Siraj-ud-Daula results in British soldiers being imprisoned in the notorious Black Hole of Calcutta.

1757
Montcalm captures Fort William Henry. Native allies kill and scalp sick and wounded British soldiers supposedly under French protection.

1758
Fort Duquesne falls to the British, who build their own stronghold, Fort Pitt (Pittsburgh).

1758
The Nova Scotia provincial parliament, the oldest legislative assembly in Canada, begins.

Girty and His Times	*Canada and the World*
	British troops capture Louisbourg for a second time, and this time destroy it.
	Montcalm defeats British at Carillon (Ticonderoga).
	1759 General James Wolfe defeats Montcalm on the Plains of Abraham. The British capture Quebec. Both generals are killed.
	Voltaire's novel *Candide* is published.
	1760 The British capture Montreal. General James Murray becomes the first British military governor of Quebec.
	George III becomes King of England.
1761 Mary Girty-Turner is returned to white society.	
1763 Guyasuta and Senecas join Pontiac's War against the British. Simon is not required to fight against white people. The King's Proclamation of 1763 — one of the principal causes	**1763** The Seven Years' War ends in British victory. Canada formally becomes a British colony. Ottawa Chief Pontiac leads a Native war against the British.

Girty and His Times	*Canada and the World*

of the American Revolution —
establishes a boundary between
white settlements and Native
lands.

1764
November 14: Simon is returned
to white society as part of an
overall surrendering of captives.
He is reunited with brother
James and forms a friendship
with Alexander McKee. Later,
at Squirrel Hill near Fort Pitt,
Simon and James are welcomed
into the home of their brother
Thomas, where they also find
their mother and brother George.

1764 ►
British government passes the
first of a series of acts designed
to make the Thirteen Colonies
pay some of the cost of the Seven
Years' War. Colonists make first
objections to taxation without
representation.

1765
May: John Turner Jr. is returned
from captivity.

Pontiac's War ends. Simon meets
George Morgan and Matthew
Elliott.

1765
British parliament passes the
Stamp Act and the Quartering
Act, further antagonizing colo-
nists.

A Scottish instrument maker,
James Watt, makes the first con-
denser for a steam engine.

1768
A Shawnee war party attacks
Simon's hunting group on the
Cumberland River. Only Simon
survives.

Simon is a principal interpreter
at the Fort Stanwix Treaty talks.

1768
Sir Guy Carlton becomes
Governor of Quebec.

Samuel Adams of Massachusetts
writes a circular letter calling on
colonists to unite in their opposi-
tion against the British government.

Girty and His Times

Canada and the World

The Iroquois sell large tracts
of land to whites, angering the
Delawares and Shawnees.

1769
Simon is the principal interpreter at meeting in Pittsburgh
between the Shawnees and
Iroquois.

1770
English explorer Samuel Hearne
sets out on his Arctic expedition
to find the Coppermine River.

British troops fire on a threatening mob in what becomes known
as the Boston Massacre.

Captain James Cook claims New
Zealand for England.

1771
Samuel Hearne becomes the first
European to reach the Arctic
Ocean overland.

1772
Simon is escort and interpreter
for Guyasuta when the chief
goes to Johnson Hall to meet Sir
William Johnson.

1773
Lord Dunmore arrives at
Pittsburg and renames it Fort
Dunmore.

1773
Colonists disguised as Natives
board a ship in Boston
Harbour and throw chests of

Girty and His Times	*Canada and the World*
	tea overboard. The incident is known as the Boston Tea Party.
1774 Simon is again Guyasuta's escort and interpreter at Johnson Hall. He becomes involved in Dunmore's War, befriends Simon Kenton (going by the name Butler), and delivers Chief Logan's eloquent speech to the Americans.	**1774** The Quebec Act is passed, guaranteeing French-Canadian language and religious and civil rights. Colonial delegates hold the First Continental Congress to discuss grievances against King George III.
1775 Amidst rumours of a rebellion against Britain, Simon's name appears on Lord Dunmore's secret list of men he considers loyal to the king. Simon is hired as guide and interpreter for Captain James Woods' diplomatic mission among the tribes. At a council held at Pittsburgh, representatives of the Continental Congress promise a delegation of chiefs from the western tribes that the Americans will always honour the Ohio River as the boundary between white and Native lands.	**1775** The American Revolution begins with shooting at Lexington and Concord. Paul Revere makes his famous ride. Quebec, Nova Scotia, and Prince Edward Island decide not to join the rebellion.
1776 Alexander McKee is placed under virtual house arrest.	**1776** Fur traders in Montreal form the North West Company to

Girty and His Times

George Morgan sends Simon to the Six Nations Grand Council to convince the Iroquois chiefs to remain neutral. The mission is a success.

Morgan fires Simon under mysterious circumstances.

Simon raises a militia company, but is slighted when he is not made captain.

A rumour names Simon and McKee as conspirators in a Loyalist plot to seize Pittsburgh for the British.

1777
Simon loses Guyasuta's friendship.

1778
Simon is a reluctant participant in General Edward Hand's "Squaw Campaign."

Canada and the World

compete with the Hudson's Bay Company.
Colonial leaders sign the Declaration of Independence.

France and Spain promise to help American colonies fight Britain.

The first Loyalists arrive in Canada.

George Washington crosses the Delaware River.

1777
The Marquis de Lafayette arrives to help the Americans.

The Americans win their first major battle at Saratoga.

Congress adopts the Article of Confederation.

Washington's army goes into winter camp at Valley Forge.

1778
Captain James Cook explores the Pacific coast from Nootka, Vancouver Island, to the Bering Strait.

Girty and His Times

Simon decides to go over to the British side out of concern for the Natives, and flees from Pittsburgh with Alexander McKee and Matthew Elliott. Simon joins the British Indian Department as an agent and interpreter. James and George Girty soon follow Simon in defecting to the British.

A Pennsylvania court declares Simon, James, and George Girty to be outlaws.

Simon rescues Simon Kenton from execution by burning.

Canada and the World

France formally declares war on Britain.

1779

Simon participates in the ambush of Captain John Clark's column, participates in an attack on Fort Laurens, successfully undertakes a spy mission to Pittsburgh to retrieve documents, and participates in an attack on American boats commanded by Colonel David Rogers.

1779

Captain Cook is killed by Natives in the Hawaiian Islands.

John Paul Jones, captain of the American ship *Bonhomme Richard*, captures the British warship *Serapis*.

1780

Simon participates in the capture of Ruddles' Station and Martin's Station.

1780

Benedict Arnold turns traitor.

1781

Simon spies on the army of George Rogers Clark at the Falls of the Ohio.

1781

General Cornwallis surrenders to Washington at Yorktown.

Girty and His Times	*Canada and the World*

Simon saves Henry Baker from death by burning.

Simon participates, with Joseph Brant, in attack on river flotilla commanded by Colonel Archibald Lochry.

Following a drunken dispute, Brant strikes Simon on the head with a sword, almost killing him. Simon is in a coma for weeks.

1782
American militiamen murder ninety-six Christian Delawares in the Gnadenhutten Massacre.

Simon participates in the Battle of Sandusky, in which the army of Colonel William Crawford is routed.

Simon tries, but fails, to save Crawford from death by fire. A spurious account of Crawford's death focuses on Simon as an approving witness who taunts the dying man.

Simon participates in attack on Bryan's Station.

Simon participates in the defeat of the Kentucky militia at the Battle of Blue Licks. This was the last battle of the Revolutionary War.

Girty and His Times	*Canada and the World*
1783 Simon is instrumental in rescuing many Americans from captivity. Simon confronts Joseph Brant for the first time since the near-fatal incident and challenges him to a duel. Brant declines. Simon supports the idea of a Native confederation and works with Brant in spite of their differences.	**1783** Large numbers of Loyalists begin arriving at the mouth of the St. John River in what is now New Brunswick. The Treaty of Paris formally ends the Revolutionary War. Washington disbands his army. The border between the United States and Canada is established from the Atlantic coast to Lake of the Woods.
1784 Simon rescues Catherine Malott from captivity and later marries her. He obtains land in Canada at present day Malden, builds a house, and establishes a farm.	
1785 Simon and Catherine's first child, John, dies in infancy in the spring. Mary Girty-Turner dies on July 31.	
1786 Tribal leaders are intimidated into signing away lands through treaties such as the Treaty of Fort Finney. Native raids against Americans escalate.	**1786** The U.S. adopts a decimal monetary system based on the Spanish dollar. Mozart's opera, *The Marriage of Figaro*, is performed for the first time.

Girty and His Times

Simon's anti-American activity
among Natives is brought to the
attention of Congress.

Simon spies on George Rogers
Clark's abortive expedition.

Nancy Anne, Girty's daughter, is
born.

1788
Girty's son, Thomas, is born in
August.

1789
Arthur St. Clair persuades
Chiefs Guyasuta, Pipe, and Half
King, to sign the Fort Harmar
treaties.

1790
Simon participates in the defeat
of General Josiah Harmar in

Canada and the World

1788
There are food shortages in
France. King Louis XVI abolishes the power of parliament to
review royal edicts.

Because of overcrowded prisons,
Britain starts sending convicts to
Australia.

1789
Alexander Mackenzie follows
the Mackenzie River to the
Arctic.

George Washington becomes
the first president of the United
States. John Adams is Vice
President.

In Paris, a mob storms the
Bastille, marking the start of the
French Revolution.

1790
Benjamin Franklin dies.

Girty and His Times	*Canada and the World*
the Battle of the Pumpkin Fields.	In England, executing women for treason by burning them at the stake is abolished.
	1790 George Washington chooses the site for the new American capital.

1791
Simon likely participates in the attack on Baker's Station.

Simon is held responsible for murder of Abner Hunt, but probably wasn't present.

Simon plays a leading part in the defeat of General Arthur St. Clair at the Battle of the Wabash.

1791
Because of the arrival of many more Loyalists, the colony of Quebec is divided into Upper and Lower Canada, each with its own assembly.

Louis XVI and his queen, Marie Antoinette, are arrested attempting to flee from France.

The U.S. Bill of Rights is ratified.

1792
General "Mad Anthony" Wayne is chosen to build and lead a new American army in the west.

Simon is the only white man allowed to attend Native council at The Glaize.

Chiefs insist on keeping the Ohio River as the boundary between their country and the United States.

Simon probably goes to Pittsburgh in disguise on a spy mission.

1792
Captain George Vancouver begins charting the coast of British Columbia and Vancouver Island.

Girty and His Times

1793
There is a split in the Native Confederation as Brant advises compromise with the Americans.

Simon is interpreter at a conference held at Malden and shows contempt for Americans by wearing a feather in his nose.

American delegates inform General Wayne of their failure to reach an agreement with the chiefs.

Simon spies on Wayne's army.

Americans place a $1,000 bounty on Simon's head.

1794
Simon participates in a failed attack on Fort Recovery.

Simon is present at the Native defeat at Fallen Timbers, but takes no part in the fighting.

Simon spends the winter assisting Native refugees.

Simon carries out his last spy mission against Americans.

Chiefs Pipe and Half King die.

Canada and the World

1793
Johns Graves Simcoe founds York (Toronto).

Alexander Mackenzie reaches the Pacific Ocean overland.

The U.S. government passes the first Fugitive Slave Act.

The Reign of Terror begins in France. Louis XVI and Marie Antoinette are executed.

1794
The United States and Great Britain sign the Jay Treaty. Britain agrees to give up western forts.

The Reign of Terror ends with the execution of Robespierre, its chief architect.

Girty and His Times

Canada and the World

1795
Natives sign Treaty of Fort
Greenville, ceding vast territory
to the U.S.

Chief Guyasuta dies.

1796
The British evacuate Detroit on
July 7.

George Girty dies.

Bredon Prideaux, Simon's son, is
born on October 20.

1796
York becomes the capital of
Upper Canada.

John Adams is elected president
of the United States.

General Anthony Wayne dies.

In England, Dr. Edward Jenner
experiments with inoculations to
fight smallpox.

1797
David Thompson leaves the
Hudson's Bay Company and joins
the North West Company.

1798
Catherine leaves Simon because
of his heavy drinking.

1798
Napoleon invades Egypt.

Admiral Nelson defeats French
fleet in the Battle of the Nile.

1799
Alexander McKee dies in January.

1799
George Washington dies.

1800
Simon is injured in a fall and is
left with a permanent limp.

1800
The Library of Congress is
founded.

Girty and His Times	*Canada and the World*

1801
Thomas Jefferson is inaugurated as president of the United States.

Napoleon defeats Austria.

1802
General Isaac Brock arrives in Canada.

1803
Ohio becomes the seventeenth U.S. state.
The U.S. government purchases Louisiana Territory from Napoleon.

1804
Aaron Burr kills Alexander Hamilton in a duel.

The Lewis and Clark expedition begins.

Napoleon crowns himself emperor of France.

Half the population of the Hawaiian Islands dies from epidemic disease brought by Europeans.

1805
Nelson defeats the French fleet at Trafalgar, but is killed in the battle.

Girty and His Times	*Canada and the World*
1807 Joseph Brant dies on November 24.	**1807** ✓ Slavery is abolished in British North America.
	Robert Fulton sails the first steamboat on the Hudson River.
	The Embargo Act forbids Americans to engage in trade with Britain or British colonies.
	The U.S. government passes a law forbidding the importation of slaves, but the law is ignored in the southern states.
	Napoleon defeats the Russian and Prussian armies.
	1808 The first permanent lighthouse on the Great Lakes is erected on Gibraltar Point, Toronto Island.
	Simon Fraser travels 1,360 kilometres down the Fraser River to the Pacific Ocean.
	1809 James Madison is elected president of the U.S.
	Napoleon puts his brother Joseph on the throne of Spain.
1809 Thomas (son) marries and brings his bride to live in the Girty home.	**1809** Abraham Lincoln is born.

Girty and His Times	*Canada and the World*
Simon's eyesight begins to fail.	
	1810
	The United States annexes part of Spanish-owned Florida.
	King George III is declared mentally incompetent. His son George, the Prince of Wales, takes over monarch's duties as Prince Regent.
	1811
	Lord Selkirk plans a settlement for Scots in the Red River area.
	Venezuela, Bolivia, and New Grenada (Columbia) rebel against Spanish rule.
	In Mexico, Father Hidalgo is executed for leading a peasants' revolt against Spanish rulers.
	A slave revolt outside New Orleans is brutally crushed.
1812	**1812**
The War of 1812 begins.	Selkirk settlers reach the Red River.
General Brock captures Detroit with Tecumseh's help.	Brock is killed at the Battle of Queenston Heights.
James Girty is hired as interpreter, but Simon is passed over.	James Madison is re-elected.
Shawnee Chief Tecumseh visits Simon.	Charles Dickens is born.

Girty and His Times	**Canada and the World**
Thomas Girty (son) dies.	Napoleon invades Russia.

1813

Simon and Matthew Elliott flee before American invasion and go to stay with Mohawks at Burlington.

Tecumseh is killed in the Battle of Moraviantown. American reports say Simon died in the same battle.

1813

The American fleet under Oliver Hazard Perry wins the Battle of Lake Erie.

Laura Secord makes her famous walk to warn of American attack.

British/Canadian forces win battles at Stoney Creek, Beaver Dams, Crysler's Farm, and Chateauguay.

Americans capture and burn York.

Napoleon's retreat from Moscow turns into a disaster.

1814

Matthew Elliott dies on May 7.

The War of 1812 ends.

1814

British/Canadian forces win the Battle of Lundy's Lane.

British troops burn Washington, D.C.

Napoleon is exiled to the Island of Elba.

1815

Andrew Jackson defeats a large British army at New Orleans.

Napoleon returns from Elba.

Girty and His Times	**Canada and the World**
	The Duke of Wellington defeats Napoleon at the battle of Waterloo. Napoleon is exiled to the Island of St. Helena.
1816 Simon returns home and is reunited with Catherine.	**1816** Natives and Métis massacre Selkirk settlers at Seven Oaks.
	James Monroe is elected president of the U.S.
1817 James Girty dies on April 17.	**1817** The first steamboats, *Frontenac* and *Ontario*, are launched on Lake Ontario.
	The Bank of Montreal is founded.
	Great Britain and the United States sign the Rush-Bagot Treaty, limiting the number of warships on the Great Lakes.
	Harvard Law School is founded.
1818 George Rogers Clark dies on February 13. Simon dies on February 18 and is buried with military honours.	**1818** The 49th Parallel is agreed upon as the Canada–U.S. border from Lake of the Woods to the Rocky Mountains.
1820 Thomas Girty (brother) dies. Daniel Boone dies.	**1820** King George III dies. The Prince Regent is crowned King George IV.

Girty and His Times

Canada and the World

1821
The Lachine Canal is completed.

The Hudson's Bay Company
absorbs the North West
Company.

The United States buys the rest of
Florida from Spain.

Napoleon dies.

1824
The first Welland Canal is completed.

1826
John By builds the Rideau Canal.

James Fenimore Cooper's novel
Last of the Mohicans is published.

1829
Shawnandithit, last of
the Beothuk Natives of
Newfoundland, dies in St. John's.

Greece wins independence from
the Ottoman Empire.

Mexico abolishes slavery.

1830
Dawn, a community of ex-slaves
from the U.S., is founded near
Dresden, Upper Canada.

Girty and His Times	*Canada and the World*
	1836 President Andrew Jackson signs the Indian Removal Bill, which banishes the Cherokees, Creeks, and other eastern tribes to lands west of the Mississippi River.
	King George IV dies. His brother inherits the crown as King William IV.
	1831 The first Natives to be forcibly removed from their traditional lands set out on a journey that will become known as The Trail of Tears. These expulsions will continue until 1838.
	1834 York is renamed Toronto. William Lyon Mackenzie is the city's first mayor.
	Slavery is abolished throughout the British Empire.
1836 Simon Kenton dies.	**1836** The first railway in Canada runs between La Prairie and Saint-Jean-sur-Richelieu.
	The Mexican army massacres the garrison of the Alamo in San Antonio, Texas.

Girty and His Times	*Canada and the World*
	1837 Rebellions in Upper and Lower Canada are led by William Lyon Mackenzie and Louis Joseph Papineau.
	Samuel Morse patents the telegraph.
	King William IV dies.
	Queen Victoria ascends the throne. The beginning of the Victorian Age.
	1839 Lord Durham recommends responsible government and the union of Upper and Lower Canada.
1840 John Turner Jr. (half-brother) dies.	
	1841 The Act of Union unites Upper and Lower Canada into single Province of Canada, to be called Canada West and Canada East.
	Britain makes New Zealand a colony.
	1843 Victoria is founded on Vancouver Island.

Girty and His Times	*Canada and the World*
	Britain bans gibbeting — publicly hanging in chains the bodies of executed criminals.
	1845 The Franklin Expedition vanishes in the Arctic while searching for the Northwest Passage.
	1849 The Amnesty Act allows William Lyon Mackenzie to return to Canada from exile in the U.S.
	The California Gold Rush begins.
1852 Catherine Malott Girty (widow) dies.	**1852** Laval University is founded.
	Harriet Beecher Stowe's anti-slavery novel, *Uncle Tom's Cabin*, is published.

Bibliography

Abernethy, Thomas. *Western Lands and the American Revolution.* New York: Russel & Russel, 1959.

Boatner, Mark, ed. *Encyclopedia of the American Revolution.* New York: David McKay Co., 1966.

Boyd, Thomas. *Simon Girty: The White Savage.* New York: Minton, Balch & Co., 1928.

Butterfield, Consul Willshire. *History of the Girtys.* Cincinnati, Ohio: Robert Clark & Co., 1890.

Coffin, Tristram Potter. *Uncertain Glory.* Detroit: Gale Group, 1971.

Dupuy, Trevor, and Gay Hammerman. *People and Events of the American Revolution.* New York: R.R. Bowker & Company, 1974.

Eckert, Allan W. *A Sorrow in Our Heart: The Life of Tecumseh.* New York: Bantam Books, 1992.

Fuller, R.M. *Windsor Heritage.* Windsor, Ontario: Herald Press, 1972.

Heckewelder, John, *A Narrative of the Mission of the United Brethren among the Delaware and Mohegan Indians from its Commencement in the Year 1740 to the Close of the Year 1808.* Philadelphia: M'Carty & Davis, 1820.

Hoffman, Phillip W. *Simon Girty: Turncoat Hero.* Franklin, Tennessee: American History Press, 2008.

Kelsey, Isabel Thompson. *Joseph Brant, 1743–1807, Man of Two Worlds.* Syracuse, New York: Syracuse University Press, 1984.

Roosevelt, Theodore. *The Winning of the West.* 4 vols. New York: G.P. Putnam's Sons, 1896–1899.

Van Every, Dale. *A Company of Heroes: The American Frontier, 1775–1783.* New York: Arno Press, 1977.

Index